the Pony

SBN 361 02035 X
Published by Purnell Books, Berkshire House, Queen Street, Maide
Copyright © 1974 PURNELL & SONS LTD.
Made and printed in Great Britain by
Purnell & Sons Ltd., Paulton (Somerset) and London

Club annual

PURNELL

Contents

Laura sat on the steps of the garden shed playing with Polly's cat. What a noise there was coming from the cottage! The clink of dishes and Polly's lively chatter from the kitchen window; the blare of Gary Glitter coming from the sitting-room where Polly's brother Ted was having a one-man disco; the sound of drawers opening and shutting upstairs. The noises were hardly in tune with each other—in fact it was a kind of stereophonic nightmare. Yet, in a funny way, they did blend together to make a homely, family sound that Laura liked.

She had only known Polly for a few days. Her family had just moved to Warwickshire from London. It had been awful to be thrown into a huge comprehensive school in the middle of term. Polly had rescued her as she wandered

Night Visitors

By Selina Charlton

Illustrated by Carolyn Dinan

helplessly round the great dining-room, looking for her dinner queue. She felt so shy she would rather have starved than ask anyone what to do. She and Polly had become friends immediately and were delighted to find that they lived in neighbouring villages, only a mile and a half apart.

"Funny to think I was frightened of meeting Polly's family," thought Laura, tickling the cat absent-mindedly behind the ear. Her own parents were both artists working at home and she had no brothers and sisters. As she thought of her home, the back kitchen door of the cottage burst open and Polly came out, laughing.

"Father just asked where that nice girl was I brought home to tea. He wondered if we'd frightened you away with our noise!"

"I'm fine. I rather like the noise. But I must be off now—it's getting dark already."

They went into the house to get their coats. Laura stood shyly in the hall as Polly opened the sitting-room door. "Can't you turn it DOWN?" she shouted to her brother Ted, who was sitting with his legs dangling over the edge of an armchair, tuning his guitar to the record.

"Just let me get this bit right first," he yelled cheerfully above the noise. "Cheerio, Laura. Come again, and bring your earplugs!"

Laughing, they went round the back to get Polly's bike. "I've still got the nicest thing to show you," said Polly. "Now you've met all my family you must meet our horses, Gilbert and Sapphira. Gilbert's mine and Sapphira belongs to Ted. Come on, they're in a field right on your way home."

The two girls strode off down the street together. They were both the same age— thirteen—but it would have been hard to find two more different girls. Where Laura was fair and quiet, Polly was dark and exuberant. Her deep, brown curls framed dark eyes and a quick smile. She was stockily built and liked bright colours and mad fashions. At the moment she wore a red shirt, blue jeans with flares and an old denim bomber jacket of Ted's with a butterfly patch on one pocket, a rabbit eating a carrot on the other and THIS WAY UP sewn upside down on the back. Laura wore a neat blue shirt, white socks and green anorak. She was small and slight with wispy blonde hair and a heart-shaped face. She looked so pale and serious, her new friend would have been surprised to know how happy she was feeling as they walked along.

"Why do you keep the horses so far out?" asked Laura, flagging a little.

"We used to have a field in the village but it was sold for building. Nobody seems to want horses—they're such fussy eaters—they won't graze the long grass. Then Mr Gillespie let us have a two-acre paddock about a mile out of the village. It'll be good because it's halfway between your village and mine. I don't really think he wanted us, but Father teaches his children and I think he felt sorry for us. Sometimes I wonder if he isn't beginning to regret taking pity on us— he used to be so nice to us but lately he's been getting fussier and fussier."

It was a lonely road and very dark. At last Polly stopped. "Here we are! Hold my bike and I'll give Gilbert a whistle."

There was a thundering noise and two enormous shapes came galloping towards the gate.

"Which one is Gilbert?" asked Laura, nervously.

"He's the handsome one. Aren't you, boy." She rubbed the velvet nose of a bay cob, about 15 hands high with a long white blaze and white socks. "I called him after Gilbert O'Sullivan because he's got such a kind face."

"You are daft," giggled Laura. By the light of Polly's bike lamp she looked at the two horses. Gilbert was a gentle, reliable-looking sort; but although she would never have admitted it to his doting owner, it was Sapphira who really impressed her. She was a light hunter, about 15.2 hands, long-legged with a thoroughbred head. Her dark, luminous eyes shone in the lamplight; her grey coat showed silver with deeper grey dapples. She was beautiful!

Laura looked at her watch. "Help! I'd better get home. I promised to be in by eight."

"I'll just check the gate. Mr Gillespie worries in case his cattle should get through our field and on to the road. It's not very likely—there's a railway embankment between us and the rest of his fields, so they'd have to get through their field gate and then under the old railway arch before they reached our field. I think it's probably because he can't see us from his farmhouse that he worries so much what we're doing down here. We're being extra careful. If we lost this field I don't know what we'd do."

Calling good-night to the horses, they carried on the last half-mile to Laura's home. "You will come over on Saturday, won't you?" begged Polly. "We can go turn and turn about on Gilbert and the bike. There's loads of lovely rides round here."

"I'd love to," said Laura. "But I've only ridden a little in riding-schools before. My last two rides were horrible: we just slopped along, nose to tail, and the girl was so bad-tempered. It's put me off riding a bit."

"Well, riding shouldn't be like that," said Polly indignantly. "When you come on Saturday and ride Gilbert you'll see how different it will be. You've just come across two very bad schools. One day I'll take you to meet my friend Mrs Ross. She owns the school where I learnt to ride. The horses have proper rest days and she keeps them fit and interested."

All Laura's doubts vanished over the next few weeks. Soon she was completely bitten by the riding bug and her parents were complaining that they never saw her. Even though it got dark so early, she and Ted and Polly met most evenings at the stable. Laura began to feel she had known them all her life. She grew fond of the steady Gilbert, though she still longed for a chance to ride Sapphira.

Then one glorious evening Ted said casually, "Like to have a go on Sappy? Steady though, she's liable to do the ton if you don't watch her. Hey—whoa! You'll have to take care of that grin of yours; your face'll fall in half!"

Saturdays became golden days for Laura. The plans for the rock group were taking up more and more of Ted's time. Or were they really? Perhaps he was just pretending they were so that Sapphira would be free for her to ride. Ted was a funny mixture, thought Laura. He was adept at coming into the kitchen and saying brightly "Can I help?" just as she and Polly put away the last spoon. Yet he painstakingly helped her to improve her seat and spent hours, when he could have been riding himself, teaching her to jump and do basic dressage.

Laura had never been so happy. But there was just one thing that spoilt her blissful weekends. As October turned into November Mr Gillespie was getting more and more bad-tempered with them. The most trivial things seemed to annoy him. Several weeks running there was a bedraggled note on the stable door when they arrived.

"Please move muckheap. It is getting too large." Then another time: "Do not leave gate open even while you are in field. Keep shut at all times." Or: "If horses weaken hedge by gate any further I must ask you to get wire replaced."

One day Ted lost his temper. "It's like having the Gestapo up there on the hill, spying on us all the time. I wish he'd come and have it out with us instead of lurking about leaving notes!"

Ted soon had his wish; but it was poor Laura who had to face Mr Gillespie when he did come. Early one bright, Saturday morning Laura had arranged to help Ted get Sapphira ready for a pony club rally. Even though she was only going on the bike to watch, she was especially happy that day: the rally was being held at Mrs Ross's stable and at last she would have the chance to meet Polly's old teacher. She came down to earth with a bump as she met a very angry Mr Gillespie outside the field gate.

"I've been waiting for one of you to turn up," he stormed. "Now look here, Laura, this has got to stop. Hordes of you down here larking about is one thing, but letting your friends drive into the field on motor-bikes and smoke in the stable is going too far!"

"I don't understand what you mean," said Laura in a frightened voice, all her new confidence evaporating.

"Come and look here then—wheel-marks across the field. And look here, cigarette ends in the stall. There's some more over by the bridge. There's even one right the other side of the bridge up near my cattle. Now tell me you don't know what I mean!"

"I'm sorry, Mr Gillespie, but Ted doesn't smoke and he can't even ride a motor-bike. And no one comes down here except us—it's too far for the others and, anyway, they're not interested in horses."

Something in Laura's face must have convinced the farmer. "I believe you," he said grudgingly. "But someone was down here last night. I heard the bike about eleven o'clock, just as I was getting into bed. I always knew this stable would be like a magnet to you youngsters, even if you do say you don't know which of your friends it was. This is only a small farm and I've got my new Continental cattle to think about. I bought a small herd of Chianinas from Italy—only a bull and a few cows, but they're worth a fortune. My first calves are due this week, so you can imagine how I feel worrying that there might be teenagers down here charging about on motor-bikes. I know it's going to be hard for you all, but you'll have to tell the others to find some-where else to keep their horses."

Mr Gillespie walked off through the railway arch and up the long field to his farmhouse, leaving a miserable Laura.

A few minutes later Polly arrived. She was stunned by the news. "I wish it hadn't happened today. I had such a happy thing to tell you. My parents have decided to trust Ted and I on our own for the weekend while they go to a teachers' conference. Ted said he'd rather look after the house today than tomorrow, so he wondered if you'd like to take Sappy to the rally instead of him."

"Oh, Polly, I couldn't! Ted's looked forward to it for ages."

"I know, but he really does want you to go. He said he'd rather do anything than have to cook Sunday dinner to-morrow. And he thought it would be a

11

good chance for you to get enrolled. Come on. Whatever's happened, we mustn't be late."

As they hacked to the rally they tried to stop worrying about losing the field. Nothing could spoil the beauty of the last of the autumn leaves and the smell of damp earth, broken by frost.

Laura's world seemed suddenly full of magic. To have the whole day on Sapphira; to know that Ted trusted her with his precious mare; to be riding not in a bored line of tired, jaded horses but out here in the freedom—she stood up in her stirrups.

"Isn't this a wonderful day!"

"Great!" called back Polly. "Let's forget Mr Gillespie and just enjoy it."

The road lay through several small villages, then out onto a main road.

Eventually, as they clattered through a quiet village, Polly shouted: "There's Mrs Ross's farm up on the hill. We'd better step on it; the D.C.'s a great one for starting on time."

But the rally did not start on time. It never started at all. When the girls arrived at the big white gates they were stopped by two uniformed police constables.

"Would you mind not going up to the main building, miss. If you could join the others over there." One of the constables pointed to the orchard where the other pony club members were standing around talking.

"What's the matter?" asked Polly anxiously. "I hope nothing's happened to Mrs Ross."

"I'm afraid there's been a theft up at the school, miss. While the C.I.D. are investigating we'd be grateful if you could all wait over there."

They joined the others just as Mrs Ross and the D.C. came out from the farmhouse and down the orchard. Everyone crowded round asking questions, then one of the boys, noticing Mrs Ross's pale, shocked face, found her a box to sit on.

One of the boys found her a box to sit on.

"Thank you," she said shakily. "I must admit I've had the most awful blow. I went out to the tackroom about an hour ago to let the school members in to get their ponies tacked up. I found the whole place completely cleaned out—every single decent piece of tack has been stolen."

The children gasped. "Mrs Ross, how dreadful!"

"The value of the tack is well over £2,000 and not all the stuff was mine. As you know, I keep quite a few horses at livery. So you can imagine how I feel. I was well insured, of course, but it will be a great loss replacing everything, and in the meantime, of course, I have to keep the school going somehow. I am sorry I have to spoil today for you, but the police will have to be here for some time, so I'm afraid the rally is cancelled."

Before they all left, a tall man whom Mrs Ross introduced as Detective Jackson spoke to them. "Poor Mrs Ross is not the only person to have tack stolen, and I'm afraid unless we're all careful she won't be the last. In this area alone we had eight major thefts in the last two years and a total value of £10,000 of tack has disappeared without trace.

"In 1972, at the national regional crime prevention conference, we made a special study of tack thefts and we decided most of the stuff must be going to the Continent. Well, we all know British tack is marvellous stuff—the best in the world, in fact. But we don't see why some clever people should try to cut down on overheads and running costs by stealing other people's. So we brought out a booklet which we are circulating to all riding schools. Ironically enough, our officer called here with one some months ago, but the girl he gave it to forgot to pass it on to Mrs Ross. We found it folded up behind the mirror in—of all places—the tackroom.

"So what can you all do about it? Well, for a start, however little tack you have, lock it up, especially at night, and if you have good tack, especially new gear, we suggest you get it stamped with one of these."

They crowded round as he showed them a small steel leather stamper. "Look, it won't weaken the leather—just emboss the stamp so that whoever stole it would have to cut it out to avoid identification. This would damage the tack and it wouldn't be worth selling."

As soon as the detective had gone the rally broke up. One of the girls who lived nearby invited everyone to use her field for jumping practice and they spent the afternoon holding a mock gymkhana. But the theft had upset all of them and no one could think or talk about anything else.

It was dark when Laura and Polly finally arrived back at the stable. Laura went home stiff but happy after hugging Sapphira. Polly biked wearily home, worrying about the loss of the field. She broke the news to Ted and they talked about it till after midnight. At last, bleary-eyed and depressed, they went to bed.

Sunday morning was quiet for Laura, but hectic for poor Polly. She had been so determined to do everything right while her parents were away, but the day had stumbled from disaster to disaster. The joint was underdone because she had forgotten to warm the oven first; she had melted the plastic tea-strainer trying to get lumps out of the gravy and the lemon-meringue pie was soggy, for reasons known only to itself. "What's this?" asked Ted, dribbling it off his spoon.

"Yellow Irish stew?"

In the afternoon they all met at the stable. They had only been there a few minutes when Ted noticed something odd.

"Hey, Polly! There's some more dog-ends in Sappy's stall. You haven't been having another of your secret smoke sessions, have you?"

"What a cheek! Somebody's been in our stable again. I know these weren't here yesterday evening."

They went into the tackroom to show Laura.

"What would someone be prowling round our stable for?" she asked.

"It must be the phantom tack-stealer," joked Ted. "They've got £2,000-worth of saddles and bridles from the school and now they're out for the really big kill."

"What, two old saddles!" Polly held up Gilbert's much-mended Pelham bridle. "I can just see them selling this down the Champs Elysées!"

Ted's face grew thoughtful for a minute. "Wait! That's it, of course—that's what they're after, Laura!"

"What?" begged Laura, completely taken in by his air of seriousness.

"They want my old martingale to exhibit in the Louvre. Well, it is an Old Master."

Laura pushed him off the saddle-horse. She might look frail but she was surprisingly strong. He landed upside down on the end of a broom, which flew up and clouted him round the ear.

Leaping to his feet, he charged after a squealing Laura and a mad chase followed. They scrambled over bales and in and out of the two stalls, gasping with laughter. Then the laughter tailed off into an embarrassed silence. Mr Gillespie was standing in the doorway.

Their guilty-looking faces as they realised how much noise they had been making were so comical that Mr Gillespie found himself smiling.

"I came here to bash your heads together," he said drily. "I've a cow calving tonight and it sounds like a circus down here. Well, I suppose you're only young and daft once. You'd better come with me."

Puzzled, they followed him through the railway arch and then through a small gate that led into the long thirty-acre field where most of the cattle were kept. It was quite a walk up the hill. At the top lights streamed out from the cattle-

The calf was a light biscuit colour.

yard. In a loose-box to one side a cow had just calved. They watched enchanted; the calf was light biscuit-coloured and more like a fawn than a calf. The cow stood proudly beside her, lowing softly. She was a huge animal, pure white with a long face and thick neck.

"What sort of cow is she?" asked Laura.

"You're looking at a pure-bred Chianina. They come from Italy. This little lass," he said proudly, "is my first calf— the start of my herd. She's worth £20,000 to me."

"Isn't the cow enormous!"

"If you think she's big—come and see the bull!"

He stood loose in a box across the yard. They gasped. He towered over the manger a good seven foot high at the withers. Pure white like the cow but with a big lump of fat over his shoulders that reminded them rather of pictures of water-buffalo in China.

"Gosh, I wouldn't like to meet him on a dark night!" exclaimed Laura.

"He's as docile as an old donkey," laughed Mr Gillespie. "We don't even need to keep him tied. He's less trouble than the cows."

"I can see now why you worry about us so much," said Ted thoughtfully. "I'm sorry if our noise has upset you—you must have had enough on your plate with all this at stake."

"I am sorry you've got to move, though. Those are really nice horses of yours. I like seeing them about. But I just can't take risks. Soon I'll have calves all over the place. It just needs the gate to be left open or someone's dog up here and I might lose hundreds of pounds worth of stock. But I hope we'll part friends. I'm sorry if worry made me a bit sharp the other day. I'll put in a good word for you round about."

Laura had to go home early, to wash her hair ready for school. Polly returned to her chores and Ted to his guitar. Late in the evening, the phone rang and Ted answered it. "It's Laura," said a frantic voice. "Can you hear me? I've got to whisper 'cos everyone's in bed and they think I am too. Can I come round?"

"What's the matter?" asked Ted, anxiously.

"I can't explain," she sobbed. "But I've done something daft and I wondered if you could help me."

"Leave a note on your pillow to say where you are just in case anyone looks in and gets worried. Start out and I'll meet you." He put down the phone and was off like a shot, offering no explanation to his surprised sister.

He came back, twenty minutes later, with a shivering Laura. She stood pathetically on the doorstep, looking quite normal except that her hair was tied up in a scarf and her eyes were puffy with crying.

"It's her hair," exclaimed Ted, standing behind her and making signals at Polly not to laugh. Laura unrolled the headscarf. Her friend gasped. The whole of her front hair was streaked with red and green patches.

"Laura, what have you done?" cried Polly.

"Please don't laugh," she wailed. "I was fooling about after I washed it and I tried out the David Bowie look with felt pens. Only it won't come off and it's school tomorrow. My mother'll go mad when she sees it!"

"What have you tried?" asked the ever-practical Polly.

"Shampoo. Fairy Liquid. It just won't come out. I daren't try anything stronger."

"Hmm. Turps would strip all the natural colour out as well. Hang on. Mother has some meths and soap-flakes mixed up in a bottle. I've seen her wash blankets with it—so it's sure to be o.k. for hair. Honestly, you're too daft for words!"

Ted soaked some cotton-wool in the mixture and gingerly tried it on her hair. Soon the table was covered with red and

Two men climbed over the gate.

green cotton-wool and her hair was back
to normal.

"Phew! You had me worried there for
a minute," said Ted. "I didn't want the
love of my life looking like Yul Brynner.
I mean, a face like a flute is one thing.
But a face like a flute and a bald bonce
is quite another! Come on, we'll smuggle
you back home."

It was a lovely night, crisp and starry
with luminous wisps of cloud that
seemed to hang in space. They walked
along, chatting and laughing for a while,
and then, as if by unspoken agreement,
they all fell silent.

It came as a complete shock when they
heard the motor-bike. The sudden noise
was like machine-gun fire in the still-
ness. For a few moments they could
follow the noise coming towards them.
Then it stopped abruptly somewhere up
ahead.

Ted caught Laura's arm. "Someone's
up by our stable again. It must be the
same ones that left the fag-ends and the
tyre-marks. You know, the phantom tack-
stealers."

"Don't be silly, Ted. You know we were
only joking. They couldn't possibly be

16

after our old stuff."

"Well, let's find out what they have been after. If we go through the hedge here we can cut across the next field and come to the railway arch. We can hide there and see what's going on."

Scratched and muddy, they reached the arch and stood in the shadows, trying not to make a sound. Ted left the two girls and, keeping below the line of vision, crept over to the stables. He was back within minutes. "There's two men there," he hissed urgently. "They've left their bike just inside the gate. I can't catch what they're saying. Watch out — they're coming this way!"

It was difficult stumbling through the mud without making a noise; at last they reached the cover of a hedge halfway up the long field, just in time to see the two men emerge from the railway arch and climb over the gate into the long field. Laura thought they could only be heading for the farm buildings at the top of the field. Surely if they had an honest reason for being there they would have had a torch and been walking normally; but they walked stealthily, without exchanging a word. As they got nearer the still shapes of the farm buildings they stopped as if to satisfy themselves that no one had heard them.

The children had followed without being detected. Now they watched anxiously from behind a straw-stack as the two men went into the box where, earlier in the day, Mr Gillespie had shown them the calf. They opened the top of the half-door and looked over. For a few seconds one of the men flashed a torch into the box, then snapped it off again. Then, as silently as they had come, they went back down the hill to the stable.

"Now we know what they're after,"
said Ted excitedly as they returned to the safety of the bridge. "They're cattle-rustlers; they mean to steal that calf."

"I'm shorter than you, Ted," said Laura, her eyes shining with excitement. "Let me try and creep round to the other side of the stable. If I can get behind the bales I bet I can hear what they're saying. Look, you can see where they are — there are two cigarettes glowing by Sapphira's stall."

Ted protested, but Laura had already slipped off into the darkness. They waited in suspense, unable to see or hear anything except those two red glowing dots in the stable. Just as they'd given Laura up, she popped up beside them again.

"Gilbert nearly gave me away — he's standing round the back of the stable and he whinnied when he saw me. But I managed to crouch there long enough to hear the lot! They're going back to town for an hour to wait till they can be certain Mr Gillespie's gone to bed. Then they're coming back with a van to fetch the calf. They said something about the cow kicking up a fuss. So they're going to bring a head-collar and lead her down the hill so the calf will follow. Then they're going to muzzle the cow and leave her tied in our stable."

As soon as they heard the motor-bike roar off they ran up the hill to warn Mr Gillespie.

When it comes to it, Laura was thinking from her vantage point across the yard from the loose-box where the calf had been a little time before, I feel almost sorry for the rustlers.

The two men were coming up the hill now; you could only hear them if, like Ted, Laura, Polly, Mr Gillespie and the two constables from rural patrol (hidden

17

in the barn next door), you knew that they were coming.

Yes, they'd done a very good, thorough job on organising their outing tonight, Laura thought. They had gone to so much trouble to check the calf was born and "find" a Ford Transit van in a car-park that morning just the right size for their little bit of light removals. It was almost a shame that they had such a shock waiting for them in the box.

The two men gave a last quick look round before opening the box door. Then, although they were fully prepared for it, the watchers nearly jumped out of their skins as two terrified yells came from the silent box. Instead of the doe-like cow and and her little calf the huge Chianina bull lumbered out at them from the darkness at the back of the box. They weren't to

know he was "as docile as an old donkey". They only saw a ton of muscle and bone towering over them.

They were still in a state of shock when Constable Andy Peters and Constable Norton led them gently round the corner to the waiting Panda car.

"Aren't you the young ladies I met yesterday at Mrs Ross's?" said Constable Peters suddenly. He hadn't recognised them at first without their hard hats on. "I'd know your cheeky grin anywhere," he teased Laura. "Do you two do a lot of detective work then? We've got a great future for mounted lady detectives, you know. Joking apart, I've good news for you—we've got a very strong lead on that tack theft. A man was caught trying to sell a saddle in the cattle market the same afternoon—so they weren't going

The huge bull lumbered out at them.

18

to France after all. Some of our thieves just aren't Common Market minded yet. I think we'd better borrow you three as rural patrol specials. You certainly know when to keep your eyes open!"

The two constables helped the rustlers into the back of the blue and white Escort. Winking at Laura and Polly, Constable Peters picked up the two-way radio to make his report.

"This is rural patrol Section 3, Constable Peters to Dodge City, over."

"You what, Andy?" asked a surprised voice at the other end.

"This is Constable Peters," repeated the young policeman. "Am bringing in rustlers. Please notify H.Q. I expect promotion to sheriff, over."

"Just make sure your stetson's on straight, Andy," came back the terse reply over the crackling radio. "We can see your head's swelling from here!"

"They're just jealous," grinned Andy. "No one's ever had a real live rustler on this range before."

He started the engine and the children waved as the rural patrol car cruised quietly off down the farm drive.

Ted looked at his watch and gasped "It's one o'clock!" He looked anxiously at Laura. "I hope no one's missed you —they'll be frantic. I must get you home."

"Please wait a minute." It was Mr Gillespie who had just come over from the loose-box, where he had settled the bull for the night. "You can't go without letting me say how sorry I am. There I was swearing away at you—silly the conclusions you jump to. I really did think it was you teenagers down there. Never thought for a moment it might be rustlers. That was about the only thing I didn't imagine was going to happen to my precious cattle! You see, the silly thing is those men wouldn't have been any better off stealing my calf than an

ordinary one. They must have heard someone talking in the market about the project I had here and that the calves would be worth huge sums when they were born. What they didn't realise was that they couldn't just sell them on the open market without pedigree certificates that would lead the buyer back to me. So the calf was only worth the ordinary slaughter price to the rustlers.

"But the value of that calf to me was quite another matter. The loss would have been enormous. As a breeding heifer, I will have to pay about £750 a year just to insure her. So you can imagine what a dim view my insurers would take of a claim for rustling! I owe you a lot. I hope you'll forget all the hard things I've said and carry on keeping the horses down the hill."

"That's wonderful!" said all three at once. Then Ted started to say something, hesitated and started again. "Mr Gillespie, there's just one thing. Do you think you could possibly put up with two and a half horses instead of two? You see, I've always wanted to breed from Sapphira and now that Laura's here to help us I reckon we could make a good job of breaking the foal. Would you mind?"

"After all you've done for me? You must be joking," laughed the farmer. "Of course I wouldn't mind. I don't think anyone in their right mind would quarrel at having a mounted bodyguard at the foot of their field—even if it did have a maternity ward."

As they went home, tired and happy, Laura suddenly started giggling.

"What's so funny?" asked Ted.

"A few weeks ago Daddy was complaining that I wouldn't say boo to a goose. He'll never believe that I've dyed my hair red and green and helped to catch two rustlers all in the same evening!"

19

The Pony Club

Many Pony Club members in this country may be surprised to hear that Japan also has a Pony Club. When they invited Great Britain to send a team of two girls and three boys to join the fifth Inter-Pacific Rally it seemed the most wonderful opportunity. To travel to the other side of the world is exciting enough, but add to that the thrill of riding and competing on Japanese horses against teams from Australia, America, Canada, New Zealand and Japan and you will understand how lucky the selected Pony Club members considered themselves. Felicity Astley-Cooper, Julia Henriques, David Hamilton, Julian Seaman and Matthew Straker were the five and I went along too as chaperone.

We flew to Tokyo late in July and arrived during their "hot" season. Temperatures in Tokyo were never less than 85°F. and at times reached 100°F.; add to this intense humidity and you will begin to understand that an air-conditioned room or a swimming-pool was the nicest place to be.

During our whole month's stay in Japan we were entertained most generously, shown many wonderful sights, and taken thousands of miles by plane, hydrofoil, "bullet" train, and bus. But, naturally enough, we enjoyed our contacts with the horses as much as anything.

Our first experience of Japanese horses was when we were invited to take part in the opening ceremony of the Osaka Riding Club. This newly built centre is a compound of stables, arenas, and a superb clubhouse. We soon learnt that this was the pattern of riding in this country, with either privately or club-owned horses kept in central stables with all facilities immediately around them. In all the time we were in Japan we never saw "private" stables. The reason is, of course, the dense population problem; there is hardly enough room for people and houses, certainly not for horses and stables!

Soon after arriving at the riding club everyone was investigating the horses and stables and comparing methods of stable management. While most of the foods were similar to ours, supplementary minerals and vitamins were fed as routine, and bedding was on rice straw! The horses' coats all looked wonderful and it was interesting to realise that while in Japan horses for riding are always kept stabled the New Zealanders rarely keep a horse indoors at all!! The stables seemed a little smaller than those we are used to and are under a single roof, with the horses looking inwards to a central passage-way. Many horses are imported from New Zealand or Europe, and if they arrive during the "hot" season are often put into air-conditioned boxes to acclimatise gradually. We began to realise that to ride in Japan is a very expensive pastime indeed. Not only because of the high purchase price, due to transport costs, but also the upkeep and club fees.

The opening ceremony was a magnificent affair with all the local dignitaries present, a large band playing, and all our

n Japan

By Pegotty Henriques

Takahara Ranch.

national flags flying. Mounted teams paraded before the Mayor, and team captains received the key of the city on behalf of their teams! Osaka Pony Club members displayed their equestrian skills and some of the younger ones showed imported Welsh ponies of the Section B type. We were later amazed to be shown a small mountain nearby that we were told had been landscaped out of the city's garbage. It was covered with soil and in the process of being turned into a park that would eventually incorporate a varied cross-country course for the use of the riding club!

After the excitement was over, Mrs Charles Sivewright and I made Japanese

Pony Club history by examining and passing their first "A" Test candidate. Maybe it was the first "A" Test ever to be taken under outdoor floodlighting with the stable management questioned through interpreters! All the other team members were greatly interested in the result, as the successful candidate had already proved himself a most popular member of the home team. Much discussion went on as to the various ways the test was examined and we learnt that the Americans hold "A" Test weekends starting on Friday night with a get-together to relax nerves and followed by two whole days' testing!

All the teams were now longing to get

21

down to some serious riding, so it was with great excitement that we travelled into the mountain area to Takahara Ranch. We were to stay here for a week, finally competing in scrambled teams in a two-day event. The horses had been lent from all over the country and temporarily stabled at the ranch. One was allocated to each rider.

Each morning we left our hotel at five o'clock, riding before breakfast to avoid the tremendous heat of the later morning. On the whole the horses were of nice, though varied, type; several stallions were in use, and one ex-Olympic mare, Josephine, was also competing. A certain amount of lameness became evident as the week wore on, and though the horses were watched most carefully for signs of fatigue the temperature was obviously a great strain on their stamina and some were withdrawn; replacements were provided.

By and large, most people found their mounts willing, and quite good jumpers. While Japanese horsemen are more accustomed to dressage and show jumping due to lack of space, this was one of the few occasions when a cross-country course had been built. At first the horses found it rather strange, but they soon began to enjoy themselves and seemed to catch the enthusiasm of the riders.

By this time Pony Club members from all countries were becoming close friends and the problem of the language barrier with Japanese members didn't seem to bother anyone! By the first day of the competition the true spirit of the Pony Club was evident and "who won" didn't matter, but good horsemanship first was the order of the day.

The Takahara Event was held over two days. On the first there was a dressage test of Preliminary standard; this was ridden on sand before three judges, two Japanese and one American. The second day started with Roads and Tracks immediately followed by a two-mile cross-country course. This had been designed by Mikio Chiba, their International Event rider. Though it only covered a few fields, it was surprisingly varied and, while not of heavy construction or very high, certainly posed some problems. The second fence was a serious one. It was an open water going away from home and it was unfortunate that some fifteen eliminations resulted. Those who got beyond this point mostly finished the course. Matthew, riding a horse he had not previously jumped, had a very exciting round. He was going clear and well until just after the sixteenth fence when his stirrup broke! Wisely he threw the other away too and rode on towards the seventeenth, rails in front of a ditch. His horse must have felt a difference in the rider's balance and jammed on the brakes at the last moment, sliding in a begging position into the rails. This resulted somehow in the horse being upside down in the ditch with the rails over the top and locking it into position!! When eventually extricated, the girth had broken; Matthew remounted bareback and finished the course!

Horses and riders were all exhausted at the end of this phase, as by now the sun was high overhead; but after a good washing down for the horses, and ad-lib iced drinks for the riders, they managed to summon up enough energy to complete the event with the show jumping.

This, a well-designed course of twelve fences, was also ridden on sand. The Prince and Princess came all the way from Tokyo to watch, and this of course made the closing ceremony a really exciting occasion. Everyone was presented to them at an informal luncheon party afterwards and Felicity was chosen to sit and talk with them. She told us afterwards that the Princess, who spoke extremely good English, was herself a keen rider.

Now we returned to Tokyo, to ride and compete at Badji-Kohen, a superb riding centre that has been in existence since before the war. Here, beautifully laid

The majority of horses had been brought from Takahara, so most people were riding their original mounts. Unfortunately, the British, apart from David, were remounted due to unsoundness and so had only a short time to strike up a partnership before the next competition, the Nations Cup. It was during one early-morning practice period that all the teams were televised for one of the most popular programmes in Japan, an early-morning breakfast show,

Breakfast in
Olympic Village,
Tokyo.

out amongst trees and shrubs and linked by tarmac roads, are stables, huge outdoor sand arenas, grass arenas, an indoor school, and a splendid air-conditioned clubhouse overlooking this elegant compound. When looking out from the clubhouse observation roof, watching horses working amongst these park-like surroundings, it is hard to realise that one is near the centre of the busiest capital in the world.

starting at seven-thirty. We had to get up very early that morning!

Teams had been particularly asked to compete in their national riding clothes, so everyone made a great effort to look their best for this big occasion. As we had now been living out of suitcases for three weeks, things were looking rather the worse for wear; somehow stocks were washed, jackets pressed, and everyone in their way looked a credit to their

Pony Club. The Japanese looked immaculate in superbly cut breeches and lightweight blue jackets. Great Britain wore specially-made lightweight black jackets, breeches and boots, white stocks and black caps, and for cross-country they had pale blue tee shirts and dark blue crash caps. The Australians, true to their own traditions, wore jodhpurs and short boots with green sweaters. New Zealand had black jackets, breeches and boots, and black caps with thick black sweaters for the cross-country. Canada were similar to Great Britain, while America wore well-cut dark green jackets and varied headgear; some of the girls wore a plain shaped band round their neck in place of a stock. As you can imagine, though of lightweight material, our black jackets were fairly hot and fellow competitors may have got rather a shock in the changing rooms when they saw how little was worn underneath! I can't think what their stocks were pinned to!!

The first day of the Nations Cup dawned unsurprisingly hot and all teams were ready for the start at eight o'clock. As always, the opening ceremony was superbly organised, with the Prince and Princess again in attendance. The gleaming jumps on the bright grass of the Olympic arena, the military band playing and the teams parading behind the national flags were a splendid sight. This was a two-day show-jumping competition, each member jumping a round on successive days, the totals added together for a final result. The sun blistered down and the temperature rose to 100°F. After much good sport and many laughs the Americans emerged as worthy winners. Australia and New Zealand, with a tie for second place, rode a thrilling jump-off against the clock. Great Britain were, alas, unplaced due to a lack of partner-

ship with two horses on the first day resulting in elimination. The disappointments were, however, soon forgotten and a rooftop party closed the day.

It was now nearly the end of August and we were all feeling fairly tired by the heat and the travelling, so it was with great pleasure that we set out on the last stage of our journey, a week's tour of Hokkaido. This we had all been waiting for. It is the most northern of the five islands that comprise Japan and is therefore cooler. Generally considered to be the more agricultural community, it is where the bulk of the food is grown and, more important to us, where the horses

Julia Henriques.

of the island as a welcome to the Pony Clubs, we returned to the race-course to be briefed on the final competition of the tour. This was, we learned, a cross-country event over small but well-built fences around the race-course. In this competition it was necessary to complete the course at as near as possible a speed of 400 metres per minute. Watches and stopwatches were disallowed. The horses were drawn for with scrupulous fairness and, as at all other events, the planning was meticulous.

It was sad for the organisers that the day of the event was very wet, but perhaps the more familiar weather improved the British chances! Despite the going proving rather treacherous, there were several clear rounds and we all realised that an accurate time would be the deciding factor. Absolutely soaked, and for the first time actually cold, we all adjourned to the race-course dining-room, and at a magnificent buffet luncheon Julia was announced the lucky winner. Other teams seemed used to the idea of riding accurately to time and British team members all felt the idea had possibilities in this country and might solve the problem of people going at a mad gallop round courses in order to make quite sure they were not slow!!

After a few more days on this lovely island we suddenly realised that our time in Japan was nearly over and the sad farewells began. What a month we had spent and what opportunities we had been given! None of us will forget the fun we had or the sights we saw: the volcanoes, pearl divers, or geisha girls. But, above all, we will remember the friends we made and the discovery that the spirit of the Pony Club exists throughout the world.

are bred and reared.

We were flown to the island and given a tremendous welcome at the airport by the local Pony Club. Here their activities were based on the race-course at Sapporo and our first morning was spent parading mounted through the streets and riding into the foothills to the site of the 1972 Winter Olympics. We gazed up at the largest of the two ski jumps and wondered how anyone could descend without wings! The long procession of horses returned again to the race-course, causing, it seemed to us, the most dreadful traffic congestion with police cars holding up traffic at every cross-roads! Television cameras followed everywhere. After a barbecue luncheon given by the governor

1975 Competition

Once again the top prize (in both age groups) is a fortnight's holiday at a residential riding school, up to a cost of £60. The winners in each section (seniors aged 13 to 16; juniors aged 12 and under) will be given this amount for a two-week instructional course at a residential riding school of their choice. For the runners-up there will be twenty prizes of £1 postal orders (ten in each section).

What you have to do. Firstly, look carefully at the parts marked on the diagram. These are numbered 1 to 6, and your task is to say which parts of the horse's foot are indicated. For instance, if you thought number 1 marked the frog (which it obviously doesn't) you would write "1. Frog"—and so on.

Secondly, study the list of points headed "Good Feeding" and decide which you consider the most important. You have to list them all in order of importance —for example, if you considered "Feed good quality forage" the most important, write "1. C"—and so on down to 6.

Lastly, write a Pony Club limerick starting with the line: "There was a wild pony called Star." If there is a tie, the limerick will decide the outright winner.

Entries close on 11th January 1975. They should be addressed to: Pony Club Annual Competition, Purnell Books, Berkshire House, Queen Street, Maidenhead, Berks SL6 1NF. Be sure to state your name, age and address—and to enclose the coupon which you will find on page 109.

The judges' decision is final and no correspondence will be entered into regarding this competition.

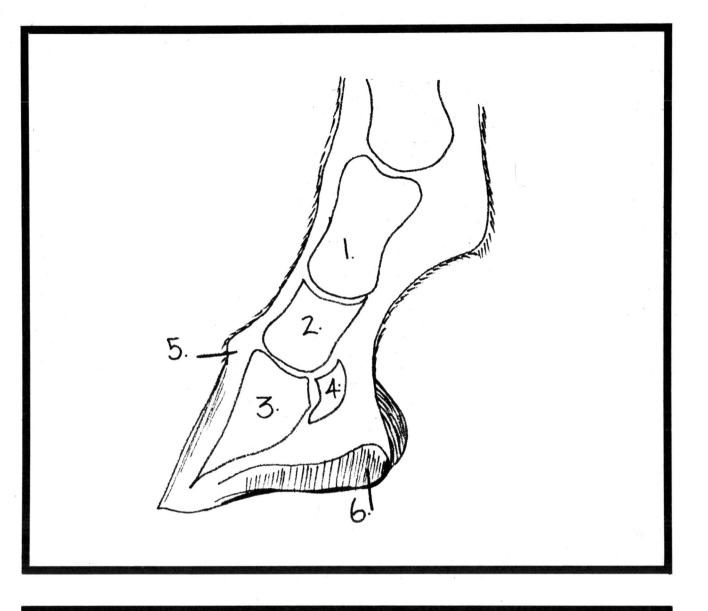

Good Feeding

A. Water before feeding.
B. Never ride immediately after a full feed.
C. Feed good quality forage.
D. Avoid sudden changes in diet.
E. Feed little and often.
F. Give plenty of bulk food.

The Strathblane team, with the Prince Philip Cup which they won for the second year running.

Pony Club

Sword race: a North Cheshire rider and a team mate.

Flag race: a member of the North Cotswold team.

A Strathblane rider in the balloon-bursting race.

Mounted Games

Sack race: two Cottesmore riders.

Grass without Tears

By Elizabeth Johnson

Illustrated by Christopher Neve

Keeping a pony at grass probably conveys a variety of meanings to different people, but let me first point out that "at grass" does not mean on the lawn in the back garden. In the broadest possible terms "at grass" means that your pony will live in a field of adequate dimensions, with the right type of fencing, a suitable supply of water, plenty of grass when available (extra feed when it is not), shelter from the worst weather and a daily visit from either yourself or a long-suffering parent.

Before going any further, there are some important questions you must ask yourself before embarking on keeping a pony and looking after it yourself. Are you prepared to spend a set time every day (and that includes holidays and Christmas Day) in attending to your pony's needs? He asks very little and will give enormous pleasure in return. Are you willing to wade through muddy areas on cold, dark nights, probably carrying a full hay net, a feed bucket and possibly water? Will you break the ice on his water tank on a really raw cold

"At Grass" does not mean on the lawn.

30

A direct path through the bullocks.

morning? Will you check his feet and shoes after they have been paddling around in wet mud all day? Can you face grooming a mud-covered pony before arriving at a pony club rally or a meet with him? If the answer to any of these questions is no, forget the pony and take up train spotting or knitting, they will suit you better and will not make so many demands on your time.

However, if you are prepared to do all the chores that are involved with keeping a pony, there is much to be remembered and learnt. In keeping a pony at grass there will be a considerable saving in time which would have to be spent exercising and keeping a stabled pony in condition. Your outdoor pony will be able to take his own exercise at will and, unless he requires stabling through ill-health, there will be no mucking out morning and evening.

Good grazing is hard to obtain unless you are lucky enough to live on a farm, as I was when I kept my first pony. But even this can have its disadvantages. On a commercial farm, the unproductive pony is merely a drain on resources and a lot of ponies will not mix well with cattle. If your pony has distinct cowboy tendencies and seems to take mischievous pleasure in herding up all the cattle, you will not be popular on the farm. Or, as in the case of my pony, he was far more subtle and would suddenly race to the far side of the field on an extremely urgent mission. His direct path happened to take it straight through the bulk of the bullocks who were peacefully asleep. On reaching his destination, the pony would turn round and innocently survey the havoc he had left behind, with forty Friesian steers cavorting madly all over the meadow. Not the best way of endearing oneself to the farmer. But not all ponies have this characteristic, many will settle quite happily with their bovine friends, but it is as well to find out before mixing the two.

For the whole year, one pony will require, ideally, 2-3 acres of grass if the grazing is to be rested at intervals. This rest period is essential, for how often does one see ponies in a bare, horse-sick pasture with little or nothing to eat except sour grass and the odd thistle or dock. Worms too are a constant source of trouble, and for a regular worming programme you should consult your veterinary surgeon. Ponies have an amazingly tough constitution and will, unfortunately, exist and work for a very long period on next to nothing. The sight of a semi-starved pony being worked hard is far too familiar. But to get the best out of your pony, the better looked after he is, the better he will perform. So having found a suitably sized field with adequate keep, your next problem will be to keep the pony in that chosen area. Starting at the top of the list, the best fencing is a solid wooden post-and-rail type. Unless you have a pony who is second cousin to a kangaroo, post and

Ponies are gregarious.

32

Don't worry if he is covered from head to foot in mud.

rails will keep all but the confirmed escapist within the bounds of the field. Also, if he does find the jumping irresistible, he is far less likely to do himself serious injury on a good solid fence. Hedges too are good protection, although ponies have an annoying habit of finding minute holes, enlarging them, and creeping out on exploratory midnight trips. There is something infinitely tempting about the neighbour's lawn or vegetable garden and so hedges should either be double fenced or very carefully checked for escape routes. It isn't that your pony is unhappy or bored with his surroundings, he is just one of nature's inquisitive creatures with a strong desire to broaden his horizons. Horses are less inquisitive; I rarely have trouble with the

big animals getting out, but ponies are invariably the ringleaders in these adventures.

If wire has to be used to fence the field, and it frequently does, it should be plain, heavy gauge and well-tensed between posts. Loose wire encourages ponies to push against it and they will soon learn how to walk through it. Barbed wire should be avoided, injuries from this dreadful invention are quite horrific and will scar for life at the very least. Patched-up fencing can be dangerous too; the moment a weak spot is noticed, it should be dealt with and not "botched up". Accidents can and do happen, however careful you may be, so any precautions are wise measures. Prevention is always better than cure.

33

A constant supply of fresh water is absolutely essential. This does not mean a couple of buckets stuck haphazardly under the fence—buckets get kicked over and are amusing playthings for a bored pony who will soon learn to play "hoof-ball" with any available object. As well as detrimental to the health (lack of water), this will also become expensive in new buckets. The only answer is a galvanised tank which will hold at least three or four days' supply of water. The best answer is a ballcock system, but these are expensive. Ponds are not suitable for drinking with the present risk of pollution. Water must always be carefully watched, both in the summer during hot weather, and in winter to remove the ice that has formed overnight. The field you choose must be inspected for odd cans, bottles and other ingredients of a rubbish tip. It is surprising how many people will shy their litter into the nearest available field, and ponies will unearth any foreign object that is lying around. As well as looking for man-made rubbish, there are other dangers in the form of poisonous plants and trees like yew, privet, ragwort, laburnum and deadly nightshade. These must be removed altogether as they can be fatal if eaten.

If your chosen field is very open and has little natural shelter, it may need some form of shed or windbreak. You may not notice your pony using the shelter, even in the coldest weather, but there may be times, often in the height of summer, when the pony wants to obtain relief from flies and hot sun. If a pony has enough food to keep him warm and happy, he will rarely need a roof over his head. But if you neglect his winter feed, he will draw on his reserves of fat to keep warm and fast lose weight and con-

dition. You may not notice this happening under a thick, woolly winter coat and what appears to be a fat, well-kept pony may turn out to be something of a hat-rack at the end of the winter. If you intend to work the pony reasonably hard at weekends, you must supplement his grazing. Certainly he will need hay in the winter, and the amount will depend on grazing available, the extent of his work and the type of pony. A small feed of nuts, chaff and carrots will also help him to keep warm and give him a little more energy during his work. Feeding quantities will vary; you should ask the advice of someone experienced in this, as each pony will require different amounts. Once feeding has begun, say in October or November, it is essential to keep a regular pattern; your pony will not appreciate a 24-hour gap when he has been used to a feed twice a day. However much you may want to settle down to your tea, remember your pony first; you will enjoy your meal far more if you know your pony is contented.

Keeping your pony with others will present problems at feeding time. Either arrange with other owners to feed at the same time or else you will have to remove your pony from the field while he eats. It is not fair to try to feed one pony with other hungry ones around—apart from this, it can be dangerous and will probably result in a kicking match. As well as food, water and shelter, your pony will require an inspection every day to check shoes, coat and general health and to look for any injury. Any sign of illness and the vet should be summoned; home treatment may only make matters worse if the trouble is at all serious. All ponies should have an anti-tetanus injection and you should keep a basic first-aid kit ready for emergencies. If you are lucky enough to have a stable, too, put your pony in it if you are waiting for the vet. Most vets are very long-suffering, but they will not appreciate a three-mile hike round and round a dark, wet field searching for the patient. In the absence of a proper stable, the garage will do, provided you remove the car and any other moveable objects like lawn mowers, old bicycles, deep freezers and anything else that has made its home in the garage. Although you may not need a rug in normal circumstances, it is useful to have some form of covering to put on your pony when he is not feeling well.

To work a pony off grass, you can have him trace-clipped and use a New Zealand rug which is waterproof and can be left on in the field. These rugs must be checked every day, preferably twice, as they can easily slip round and rub the body. It is not enough simply to glance across the field as you speed past in a car; the rug must be taken off and re-

Take no notice of the cloud of dust that seems to follow you on your ride.

placed in order to let the air circulate and to readjust the fitting.

Ponies are gregarious animals and hate being left alone, so if possible make every effort you can to share the field with at least one other horse or pony. Left on his own, a pony will fret, stand around by the gate and be altogether miserable. I have always found that ponies become bored and are far more likely to get into trouble by exploring fences and hedges when left alone. Remember too that ponies, however staid and quiet they may appear, are basically frightened of strange noises and objects. A lorry rattling past the field with a loose and noisy load may be all that is needed to set your pony galloping madly round his field, and this is the time when accidents happen.

Grooming a grass-kept pony is always a problem. Don't worry too much if every time you visit your pony he is smothered from head to foot with mud. He may look dreadful, but this is all part of his central-heating system. He will roll constantly during the winter and the extra layer of mud helps in a small way to keep him a little warmer. Do not be tempted to over-groom him either; simply remove the worst of the mud if you want to ride him, and take no notice of the cloud of dust that seems to follow you on your ride — this dust (or grease) is essential to your pony's warmth. It is not until the summer, when he loses his winter coat, that you can attempt to get rid of this. As long as his feet are well shod and you can remove the mud under his saddle and on his head, there is little else you can do about the shaggy appearance. Of course for a pony club rally or hunting you will have to make a special effort to get him looking as clean as possible, but most people who know anything about horses will understand that yours is "grass-kept".

The summer is a different matter and grooming can be carried out every day if you are riding your pony a lot. The horse world is divided into two sections, those who bath their horses and those who don't. I have always been pro-bathing in limited quantities during the summer — after a hot ride a hose down is a very good idea provided you make quite sure the pony is dry before finally turning him out. I frequently bath my horse before a show and many ponies seem to enjoy the process. My own horses enjoy it and will grab the hose-pipe between their teeth, squirting water all round the yard with scant regard for me. Too much washing will be bad for the coat but the occasional wash will do nothing but good.

As regards trimming a pony's mane and tail, this is best left to the minimum in the winter as an unpulled, longish tail (not too long so that it trails in the mud) will all help to keep the pony warm. In the summer, too, these appendages are essential to keep the flies at bay. But a long straggly mane and tail will soon become matted with mud and brambles, so they must be pulled and trimmed occasionally.

If after reading this you are still able to honestly say yes to all the queries, you are well able to care for a pony at grass. But make sure that if at any time you are ill or unable to "do" your pony, there is a willing parent or friend who can cope with the pony. The motto must always be "pony first, yourself later". One of the best books on this subject, for I have hardly scratched the surface, is the Pony Club's *Keeping a Pony at Grass*. I suggest you buy it.

Reader's Crossword

By Elaine Wingfield (age 12)

Clues

Across

1. One part in a one- or three-day event. (8)
5. Signals by the rider to direct his horse. (4)
7. Mark under saddle on ponies which have come from the moors. (5)
9. Used on roads and sometimes on horses' hooves. (3)
10. Below the fetlock. (5)
13. You can keep your horse in it. (6)
14. On the end of the leg. (4)
15. If a pony has colic he will be given this. (6)
17. A young horse. (4)
20. A horse in the year after birth. (8)
22. Abbreviation for National Hunt. (2)
23. Type of cart. (3)
25. You often do this to a young pony. (5)
26. It usually lives in an earth. (3)

Down

1. I'm strong and sturdy and live on a moor. (8)
2. Ponies and horses should have this each day. (8)
3. The saddle will fall off without this. (5)
4. Pony Club members wear a . . . . . and tie. (5)
6. Type of hunt. (4)
8. Attached to the bridle. (3)
11. Horses and ponies enjoy eating this. (3)
12. Not a stallion. (7)
14. It starts on November 1st. (7)
16. They chase the fox. (6)
17. Warble . . . . (3)
18. It switches and helps keep the flies away. (4)
21. . . . . —back. (4)
24. The side you don't mount on. (3)

Answers on page 85

Brian Fletcher and Red Rum being led in after their 1973 Grand National victory.

38

Brian Fletcher
Riders of Renown

Brian Fletcher, who was born in 1947, learnt to ride before he was able to walk. He entered his first competition at the age of nine, when he won a local "flapping" race and, for a long time afterwards, he regarded himself as the obvious successor to Gordon Richards.

His love of horses eventually drew him towards the world of steeplechasing and, at the age of sixteen, he started his career as a jockey. He still regards the thrill of riding his first winner (Grey Spirit) as one of the great highlights of his life—"I thought the world was at my feet," he says. Other memorable achievements include two Grand National victories, plus a wonderfully successful season in 1967-68, when he finished second to Josh Gifford in the steeplechase jockeys' championship.

It was after a victory at Ayr that he was offered the ride on Red Rum in the 1973 Grand National. The Australian-bred Crisp, jumping like a stag, led for most of the long journey round Aintree's enormous course, but his weight told in the end and Red Rum overhauled him on the run-in. Asked when he felt confident of winning, Brian Fletcher replied succinctly: "At the post."

He regards Red Rum as his favourite out of all the horses he has ridden —"He is a great character, he knows the thrill of victory and tries very hard for it." The latter point was proved dramatically when Brian Fletcher rode the horse in the 1973 Hennessy Cognac Gold Cup. He had to give exactly a stone in weight to Red Candle and, after a tremendous tussle, he was defeated by a short head. Like Crisp, he was hailed as one of the most gallant losers of all time.

Brian Fletcher's other great interest is farming. He likes to be occupied, enjoys the company of his young son, Andrew, and is also happy to spend time in the sauna baths—which must be a great blessing for anyone in his weight-conscious profession. His ambition is simply: "To be successful."

*Mrs Mabel Forrest on her Maeve winning the Ladies
Open race at the Morpeth Hunt Point-to-Point, 1973.*

Mrs. Mabel Forrest

Riders of Renown

Mrs Mabel Forrest was born in Scotland and has been riding virtually all her life. She was never a member of the Pony Club — "There wasn't a branch anywhere near us when I was a child" — so it was the round of local shows that provided the highlight of her summer holidays. While a teenager, she usually had three or four ponies of her own and she rode them in show-jumping classes, achieving considerable success at local level.

Her other great interest was hunting. She followed hounds at every possible opportunity during the winter months and, almost inevitably, was drawn towards the world of point-to-pointing. In 1946, when the sport resumed after the war, she had her first ride in a ladies' race; in 1950 she rode her first winner, Merely-a-Mascot. It was a memorable moment, and she regards the horse who helped her achieve it with tremendous affection. "He was a difficult ride, but he had so much character that he was always a great favourite."

By the end of the 1972 season Mabel Forrest had ridden 31 winners; the following year she pushed the total up to 48 — and won the *Sporting Life* Cup for the leading lady rider in the process. Eleven of her 1973 victories were achieved with the mare Maeve, whom she had bought as a three-year-old for a mere 200 guin-

eas; the other six were with the home-bred Dersnip. The latter had won his first race in 1972 and Mrs Forrest still regards that first victory as one of her happiest memories — "because I had bred, broken and trained him myself." In thirteen races during 1972 and 1973, Dersnip was beaten only once — and that was when he fell, while in the lead, at the final fence.

The wife of a Berwickshire farmer, Mabel Forrest finds that home and horses keep her fully occupied — but there is no hint of regret when she says that there isn't time for outside interests. She has already fulfilled her ambition to win certain specific races (among them the Middleton's four-mile ladies' race and the Goya Championship), but she would naturally enjoy winning them all again.

Janet Hodgson, winner of Burghley Horse Trials in 1972 with Larkspur.

Janet Hodgson

Riders of Renown

Janet Hodgson, who was born in 1948, had her first pony when she was only four years old. This was an eleven hands mare called Sparrow, who bit and kicked adults but was "super with children in every way". At the age of four, Janet rode Sparrow in her first competition, a leading-rein class, to finish "about fifth".

Later she became a member of the South Staffordshire branch of the Pony Club and, when an associate, she competed in the Pony Club Horse Trials Championships. Asked how she fared, her answer is brief: "Not very well!" But the sport appealed to her and the move into adult horse trials was a natural progression from Pony Club events.

She was eighteen when her father bought a "rather uncivilised" five-year-old from Ireland, whose name was Larkspur. Standing 17.1 hands high, he was a big strong novice who still had a great deal to learn. But the talent and courage were there and, when he was introduced to three-day eventing at Tidworth in 1970, he proved his worth with a fast and faultless performance across-country. Janet Hodgson regards the day that she finished her first three-day event as one of her happiest memories: "It was something I had always wanted to do."

Trained by Mrs Pearson-Adams and, more recently, by Bertie Hill, she and Larkspur had achieved a wonderfully consistent record in the major competitions before winning at Burghley in 1972. They were therefore chosen for the British team that competed in the European Championships at Kiev the following year and, though defeated, proved their combined courage as never before.

Larkspur fell at Kiev's notorious fence two; Janet Hodgson landed face down on rock-hard ground and almost lost her four front teeth in the process. Bleeding profusely, she remounted and—despite a second painful fall—she completed the course. Undeterred by her injuries, she still regards three-day eventing as her favourite sport; her other interests include hunting and reading.

Tony Newbery
Riders of Renown

Tony Newbery, a former member of the East Devon branch of the Pony Club, was born in 1953. He began riding at the age of three, on a donkey, and had his first pony—plus his first taste of the show ring—when he was six. Later, he teamed up with some of the most famous show ponies of the 1960's, among them the 13.2 hands China Tea (who won him an average of 35 first prizes each season) and the 14.2 pony Creden Lucky Charm (whose travels to 48 different shows produced 42 first prizes).

He then became involved in junior jumping and, at the age of fifteen, was selected for a junior team which went to Toronto. It was that trip which made him decide that he would concentrate on show jumping. His father therefore bought him a horse called Manx Monarch, who was an ideal "school master", and he made a highly successful transition into the Young Riders' category. His only instruction came from Bertie Hill, with whom he spent a week before the start of the 1969 and 1970 seasons.

By 1972, Tony Newbery was looking for a top-class jumper to ride in open competition. The Australian horse Warwick III was then touring the British shows and, knowing that he would be for sale at the end of the year, Tony watched his every performance with intense interest. More important, he

aroused his father's interest and eventually persuaded him to buy the horse in January 1973.

It took a month or so for the new partnership to settle down together, but, once they did, there was no holding them. Tony Newbery's greatest moment came at Aachen where, together with Alwin Schockemohle on The Robber, he finished second in the big German Grand Prix, watched by a crowd of fifty thousand people. He was then a virtually unknown nineteen-year-old, but his performances over the big tough Aachen fences made a lasting impression. At the end of the year he was chosen for the British team that toured the United States and Canada. With youth still on his side, he should be able to fulfil his ambition "to be a top-class international show jumper for as many years as possible".

45

Lucinda Prior-Palmer on Be Fair.

Lucinda Prior-Palmer

Riders of Renown

Lucinda Prior-Palmer, who was born in 1943, is a former member of the R.A. branch of the Pony Club, which she joined at the age of nine. She was chosen to represent her branch in the Pony Club Horse Trials Championships, but failed to get further than the Regional Finals — "The first time I fell off twice and eventually got eliminated!"

Her first pony was a Shetland called Risky, which she and her mother broke in and trained between them. She later progressed to larger ponies and derived enormous pleasure from riding, without collecting any hoard of rosettes. She did a little showing, with only moderate success, and failed to win any of the jumping classes or gymkhana events in which she began competing at the age of nine.

It was the chestnut gelding Be Fair who carried Lucinda Prior-Palmer into the unaccustomed limelight. She was only fifteen when her mother saw the horse advertised in *Horse and Hound* and, due to "an extraordinary extra sense", went to Birmingham and bought him. He was then a very green five-year-old, with a nasty habit of standing on his hindlegs at every opportunity. But he also had obvious talent — "We hoped that he would be capable of doing a one-day event in time," said Lucinda.

She mentions three particularly happy occasions, all of which were important landmarks in Be Fair's career. First there was her eventing debut at Rushall in 1970 — "I didn't know whether he'd go or stop, but he went brilliantly and we knew he was something." Then Badminton, 1972 — "I never expected to get round, let alone finish in fifth place." And, finally, victory at Badminton in 1973 — "A moment that could never be the same again. That sort of thing happens to everyone else, not to oneself."

Lucinda Prior-Palmer has received instruction from a number of different people — David Hunt has coached her in dressage; Pat Burgess, Lady Hugh Russell and Dick Stillwell have helped to improve her own and her horse's jumping. Horses are naturally her main interest, but she also enjoys travelling, driving and skiing (both on water and snow).

Malcolm Pyrah on Trevarrion.

48

Malcolm Pyrah
Riders of Renown

Malcolm Pyrah, a former member of the Holderness branch of the Pony Club, was born in 1941 and began riding ten years later. He competed in gymkhana events from the age of eleven and soon became quite competent, but it took him longer to master the techniques of show jumping in which he became involved the following year.

Eventually he graduated to adult jumping classes, initially riding his own horses in local shows. One of these, a horse called Dark Night, was spotted—and later bought—by the late Leonard Cawthraw. Malcolm Pyrah was asked if he would continue to ride the horse, plus the other Cawthraw jumpers that were then stabled with Trevor Banks. These included Madison Time, Lights Out and Sweep, all then in the novice grade. He gave them a good grounding, but they were passed on to other riders before making big names for themselves.

One of Malcolm Pyrah's most painful memories is connected with a show at Ostend, where he first competed as a member of the British team. "In the very first competition the horse stopped at the first fence, much to the amusement of the crowd. It seemed a bad start to my international career." But his luck was to change dramatically.

During 1972, Mrs Gascoigne wanted to buy a horse for him to ride. "I suggested Trevarrion, who was one of the few show jumpers then on the market, whereupon the mare was promptly bought." He struck up a wonderfully happy partnership with Trevarrion and the 1973 season was therefore a huge success, both at home and abroad.

Malcolm Pyrah runs a dry-cleaning business—and he enjoys the work involved. He also likes watching football and "any other first-class sport", though he hasn't the time to participate. His ambition, he says, is "to establish myself as a good horseman". Most people would say that he has done that already.

In Many

Moods

The Rally

(Impressions of a D.C.)

There's a Rally tomorrow. Oh my! Oh what fun!
The telephone's ringing, the game has begun.
Someone is saying they hope it's all right
For two of their ponies to come overnight.
One has a shoe loose, the other a cough,
If the blacksmith can't come will I take the shoe off?
Two Instructors away and the Secretary ill,
Who on earth can I find who might just fill the bill?
It's pouring with rain, the ground's like a bog,
Oh pray that it's fine, but the forecast is fog.
There are jumps to repair, and a school to lay out,
Some markers are missing I can't do without.
The measuring tape has vanished from sight,
Perhaps if I guess it will turn out all right.
The cows in the field have demolished the jumps,
The posts are all loose where they rubbed with their rumps.
There's my horse to be ridden, but too wet to saddle,
Though all we could do is to go for a paddle.
The telephone rings, an Instructor regrets
She can't come at all and *hopes* it's not wet!
If from four Branch Instructors you take away three
It only leaves one, and that one is just me.
There'll be ponies so fat that the saddle slips round,
And ponies that won't keep their nose off the ground.
Ponies too fast and ponies too slow,
Some that won't stop and some that won't go.
But big ones and small ones whatever their stride
Will all have to go in one whacking great ride.
The forecast at one says the weather is better,
But unless I'm quite blind it is getting much wetter.
I pray once again to the powers that be
To have pity for once on this hard pressed D.C.

The Rally is over, my yard's in a muck,
A hole by the gate where a horsebox got stuck;
A whip left behind and a glove in a puddle,
The stable and tack room seem all in a muddle.
But believe it or not I can honestly say
I've enjoyed every hour of this Pony Club day.

By Cdr. H. Falcon-Steward

The Fermoy Affair

By Primrose Cumming

Illustrated by Ellen Gilbert

Moving house is both sad and exciting: sad because it means saying 'goodbye' to so much, exciting because of all the new things and people and exploring to be done. And when the moving family includes two ponies and a red setter it is a pretty big upheaval.

So here we were, four Appletons, Mother, Father, Duncan, Tansy (me), bay pony Buster (Duncan's) and grey Lyric (mine) and Conker, who reckons we all belong to him, settling in at Huntley Lodge.

The house was a long white place with the usual garden and lawns, all a bit out of hand through not being lived among for a while. More interesting to Duncan and me were the stables. Where we'd come from there had been only a shed in the ponies' field and all the tack and food had to be carried there in winter through mud. But Huntley Lodge had real brick stabling with a yard and a coach-house. Dad nabbed the latter for a garage, which seemed a pity. But not having a coach, we couldn't complain, and there were places for four horses, two boxes and two stalls.

"We can have visiting horses," I said.

"It's going to take ages clearing enough space for our two," Duncan retorted.

It was a long time since the building had seen a horse. The doors of the boxes were missing, and the whole place was crammed with ancient faggots, rusted implements, stacks of waste paper and a lot more besides.

As it was summer, Buster and Lyric could be out in the orchard, but we made a start right away on clearing up. What with that and exploring the riding possibilities, we were too busy at first to notice anything odd. Looking back, Conker was the first to be affected. He never came into the stables with us, but sat outside whining while we worked. As there were mice and he was a very sporting dog, we should have taken more heed.

One day while wrestling with the faggots, which fell to bits when they were touched, I distinctly heard a snort.

"Did you make that snorting noise, Duncan?"

"Of course not. Why should I?"

I supposed I had imagined it until only a little later I heard the scraping of iron on brick. There was no mistaking the noise of a horse's impatient pawing. I was alone, for Duncan was wheeling rubbish to the bonfire, and I felt a real chill down my back. I dashed out.

"Duncan, there *is* a horse in there. I heard it again."

"Imposs! It was something on the bonfire."

"But I did, and look at Conker, he's shaking."

Duncan marched into the stables. The boxes were cleared and we were attacking the stalls where we meant to keep tack and food for the time being.

"How could there be a horse in here, unless there's a Shetland pony hiding under the rest of the junk?"

"I didn't mean a live horse."

"If there was a dead one it wouldn't . . ."

"You know very well what I mean."

"Now for heaven's sake, Tansy, don't get all psychic and start seeing ghosts. You'll be such a bore."

"I haven't seen anything," I replied. "But I've heard."

"Probably a loose tile or bargeboard. Let's take a dekko at the loft."

The loft was reached by a heavy, fixed ladder through a doorless trap. We had already ascertained it held only mouldy hay and a lot of swallows' droppings. Somehow, I felt better now that the word "ghost" was out in the open, but I let Duncan ascend alone. He soon came down again with nothing to report. A scrunch-ing outside made us both jump, but it was only Mummy.

"I've fixed your transfer to this branch of the Pony Club," she announced. "There's a working rally within hacking distance at the end of the week and Mrs Whatshername – oh, Washington – will be expecting you."

"Good-o," said Duncan. "Hope we're not too late to be picked for teams and things."

The news put thoughts of ghosts out of my mind. The one thing about the move I most dreaded was joining this new branch. You see, Lyric and I aren't at our best doing things in front of a critical audience. We kind of go to pieces if we know our approach to a jump, or which leg we're leading with, is being scrutinized too closely. The branch at our old home was small, and, I s'pose, a bit haphazard. Even the annual show was very informal and we had a lot of picnics. Occasionally a bit of an effort was made to get some frightening person along to instruct, but not too often.

Duncan used to complain about the lack of initiative, because he and Buster thirsted after rosettes. But it suited Lyric and me fine. Lyric is more intellectual than Buster and enjoys select company and beautiful views. She goes very nicely and jumps, too, so long, as I said, there aren't a lot of know-all people watching.

Duncan was yattering on: "It's got a great reputation, this branch. Been in the finals for the Prince Philip Cup and won masses of team and individual events. At last Buster will have a chance to show what he can do."

"Lyric is not an exhibitionist," I said.

"I'm sure what you and Lyric need is

Lyric stood . . . snuffling in the strangest way.

proper schooling," said Mummy. "I'm told this Mrs Washington is a very fine instructress."

My heart sank even farther. But I decided to spare no effort on the tack and grooming to make a good first impression.

Meanwhile we scrubbed out the boxes and Dad made doors out of wood salvaged from the junk. With the cobwebs down, I made a discovery.

"Look, horses' names! They must be."

The names were on boards, Steadfast and Gallant over the stalls, and Nimrod over one of the boxes.

"I bet the two in the stalls were carriage horses," said Duncan. "Nimrod must have been a hunter. I suppose they only kept the one."

"There has been a plate over the other box; there are the screw holes."

"Pr'aps they fell on hard times and had

to sell that one. Anyway, let Buster have Nimrod's box."

Duncan had fallen for the name, and as the boxes were identical, I didn't mind. That is, until I tried to lead Lyric into the other one.

We'd been longing to see the ponies in their posh new homes, so we'd put down straw on the floor and some nuts in the splendid built-in mangers. No more feeding out of buckets for our steeds!

Buster walked straight in and made unerringly for the manger. But Lyric stood teetering at the door and snuffling in the strangest way. She'd always been good about going into motor horseboxes, so I couldn't understand her behaviour now, particularly with Buster munching next door.

"Ungrateful animal, after all our trouble! Trust a mare!" scoffed Duncan.

58

After a lot of wheedling she at last stepped in. But instead of making for the manger she stared towards the blank side of the box, arching her neck and snuffing. Then she raised a forefoot and squealed, a thing she does when becoming acquainted with a new pony.

"Duncan!" I hissed. "There's a horse in here already."

"You're barmy!" But his eyes were popping.

After another little squeal, Lyric did go to the manger. But she stood close against the wall and kept turning her head and dropping bits into the straw in a maddeningly wasteful way.

"I know I'm right," I said.

"Well, she seems to have settled down with it," said Duncan, in a humouring voice. "Or do you want to swap boxes? Buster's not psychic or anything silly like that."

He was doing that psychic business to death, so I said crossly:

"There's nothing silly about Lyric. Anyhow, Buster can be aggressive. He might kick it."

"Oh, give over . . . !"

Just then Buster, having finished his nuts, came to the door, craned round to the other, put back his ears and snapped the air. Jealousy was written all over him.

"Look at that!" I said.

"He's narked because Lyric's still eating." Duncan was determined not to get rattled. "Come on, the stalls are nearly clear. Let's finish the job and leave them to settle in."

We got to work, but I had to keep taking a look. At one time Lyric had her head up and neck stretched, going through the motions of nibbling another horse's mane, only there was nothing

visible. Poor Buster was standing with his ears back looking livid.

I was certain now we had a ghost horse and Duncan would have to come round to the fact sooner or later. Could we live with it? Or, rather, could the ponies? Lyric was getting along with it fine, but it did seem hard on Buster.

Then Duncan made a find under the manger.

"The missing name board! Still got the screws in it."

The name, when the dust was rubbed off, was FERMOY.

I went to the box. Lyric stopped nibbling and came over.

"Fermoy," I called invitingly. "Fermoy!"

Lyric blew on my neck, and then there came another gust on the other side: one hot and one icy.

"It's him all right! But why's he come back and not any of the others?"

"Why was his name board taken down, yanked off pretty roughly by the splintering, and thrown away?" queried Duncan.

"He could have come to a tragic end. So tragic that his owner couldn't bear to see his name left up."

"Hunting," suggested Duncan, betraying that he was now won over. "Drowned in a flooded brook, or broke his neck at a double oxer. Pr'aps one of the locals would remember."

"Old Petemberson. He told Daddy he'd been bred and born in these parts."

We weren't sure if the pensioner who was helping tidy the garden had one long surname or had run his christian one into it. He was a dour old man, and as we were a bit shy of him we decided on a round-about approach.

"'Twasn't the last lot wot was here kept hosses, but the lot afore them," he eventually revealed. "Me Uncle Joseph worked for 'em a while."

"Were they nice ones?"

"Can't say I rightly remembers, but there wuz money."

"We found some names in the stables," I said. "Nimrod, Steadfast and Gallant. Would they have been the ones in your uncle's time?"

"Could a' bin."

Petemberson's concentration on the hedge he was chopping back became remarkably rapt and increased my suspicion that we were on a subject he did not want to discuss. I came straight to the point.

"There was a fourth that had been pulled down and thrown away: Fermoy. Why do you think that was?"

"Fer . . ." There was a noticeable break in the chopping rhythm which then became faster. "Couldn't say. I was never one for hosses. Best thing ever invented, the moty car."

We left him to his hedge.

"He knows something," I said. "But he's just not playing."

Then we learnt some more almost by accident when we went to the neighbouring farm to ask about renting extra grazing.

"So you've got ponies," said the cheerful, youngish wife. "I believe the last people to keep horses at Huntley Lodge were the Morlands."

"What were they like, the horses?" I asked at once.

"Oh, they were before my time. But they say there was a nasty accident in the stables. Young Mrs Morland had a favourite hunter and it turned vicious and kicked a groom to death."

I felt my scalp prickle and Duncan looked funny.

"What was it called?" he asked.

"I don't remember, if I ever heard. I

". . . Young Mrs Morland had a favourite hunter . . ."

60

think it was shot."

"Do-do you think the stables are haunted?" I had to ask.

"There's never been any talk of it. No, it would have been all round the village if anyone had seen anything since." She became quite concerned. "Have you seen anything?"

"No," we said together, for once of one mind—which was to keep the thing to ourselves, at least for the present.

"So we've got a vicious ghost horse," said Duncan afterwards. "Though I suppose it can't hurt if it does kick."

"Not physically," I said. "But ghosts can affect minds. S'posing it teaches Buster and Lyric to kick?"

It was a terribly worrying problem. Luckily Fermoy retired into limbo, or wherever ghosts live, for the next day or two, and we were able to work on the ponies and get them poshed up for the rally in peace.

We started off, Duncan with eagerness and I without any at all. Usually Lyric and Buster trotted along nicely together. But this morning Lyric would keep shooting ahead and then hanging to the left.

"For Pete's sake calm down, you're getting Lyric steamed up, and she's unsettling Buster," complained Duncan.

Buster, in fact, kept jibbing. Both ponies were acting right out of character, as Lyric hardly ever wanted to go ahead of Buster. A low-pitched, almost loving whicker to my right confirmed my suspicion.

"It's not me," I said. "It's Fermoy. Oh, Duncan, he's coming with us to the rally!"

"We'll just have to ignore him, that's all," said Duncan, putting on an air of firmness. "Concentrate on your riding."

There were a lot of riders at the rally, and most of them and their ponies looked so smart and competent that I shrank into my saddle. Of course, all eyes were on us, the only new-comers. In actual fact they were all prepared to be friendly, and Duncan was soon chatting away. But with the problem of Fermoy added to my shyness, I felt as dumb as I looked.

A tall, reddish woman strode up and said heartily: "You must be Tansy and Duncan Appleton. I'm Mrs Washington. Nice ponies."

She patted Buster and went to do the same to Lyric. But her hand stopped in mid-air and a queer expression flitted across her face. I guessed that Fermoy was standing in the way.

"Well, join in with the junior ride," she went on with rather forced briskness now. "We'll see how they shape."

There were about fifteen in the ride, and I prayed that Lyric and I wouldn't attract much attention. Lyric, bless her, didn't put a foot wrong, but the ride itself became disorganized from the start. None of the ponies would settle down, and a huge gap was left all round Lyric, despite Mrs Washington's efforts.

"Diana, don't leave such a gap. Use your legs. Richard, keep back, you're getting on top of Ann."

This sort of thing went on for about fifteen minutes. It was plain to me and Duncan, who was quietly having hysterics, that Fermoy was making his presence felt.

At last Mrs Washington, looking even redder, halted us and announced jumping practice. Not knowing what part Fermoy might play in this, I edged Lyric away behind the others with the idea of being a spectator. No luck.

"Where are you going, Tansy?"

"I thought I'd just watch to begin with."

"Nonsense! You can learn best by taking part. We'll start over the caveletti, then if your pony is sticky she'll follow the others."

A competent sort of girl, Joanna, was selected to go first, and Lyric and I tagged on at the end. But Joanna, looking amazed, could not get her pony up to the first bar. The others tried after her in turn, with the same lack of success. Duncan got Buster over the first two, then he shied out to the right. The more the ponies were urged, the worse they got, until one girl was tossed off by a combined shy and buck and another was bolted off with back to her trailer.

"What's got into them?" was the general wail.

"It's just as if the caveletti were haunted," observed a young boy.

He was right, of course. Fermoy must have planted himself somewhere along the line. I decided to see if he'd let Lyric go. She trotted over them perfectly, jumping the last, higher one. The others followed and we went round several times with, presumably, Fermoy leading.

"Well done, Tansy, very good!" applauded Mrs Washington.

But she looked at us somewhat oddly.

After that we did some show jumping and a small cross-country course. Except for a few, to the riders, inexplicable refusals, Fermoy did not make his presence too much felt. And encouraged by our good start over the caveletti, Lyric and I went well enough not to provoke criticism. Buster went like a bomb.

By the end of the rally I felt we had been "accepted". Quite a few people seemed to want to get to know us better, and Mrs Washington made quite a speech.

"You've got two very useful ponies . . . an asset to the branch. I'm sorry things were a bit haywire at first . . . ponies tend to be at sixes and sevens at the start of the holidays . . . soon settle down."

"So much for your fears, Tansy," chuckled Duncan as we rode home.

"It was only through Fermoy that we got off to such a good start. But, Duncan, it can't go on. I mean, if he insists on always coming anything could happen. Some wretched kid could have a bad fall through him."

"He could become a real nuisance, I suppose. But how can we stop him?"

As Fermoy seemed to have called it a day, I was able to have a hard think on the ride home.

Huntley Lodge having no reputation of being haunted, Fermoy's ghost must have been "raised" by the presence of our ponies—Lyric, perhaps because she was the mare, being the special attraction. What the farmer's wife had told us about him, for I was sure he was the horse, was extremely off putting. How terrible it must have been for young Mrs Morland to have her favourite figure

A huge gap was left all round Lyric.

in a double tragedy! If she had loved him, it seemed unlikely that he had always been vicious. Did he go suddenly berserk when he killed that groom?

In spite of the problems his "walkings" raised, I could not feel anything vicious or horrific about him. More as if he were trying to get something through to us in the way horses do when they want to attract our attention to a personal trouble.

I made my ponderings known to Duncan.

"Ghosts usually walk when a wrong has been done to them," he mused. "So you'd think it would be the groom, not Fermoy, who paid the price for his crime."

"Pr'aps he was a cruel man and provoked Fermoy. Oh, I wish we could find out exactly what happened in the stable!"

"I think Petemberson knows. It stuck out a mile he didn't want to be questioned. Pr'aps it was his uncle who died."

"He's never been near the stables all the time he's worked for us. In fact, when Daddy wanted him to deal with that creeper, he was almost fierce about it being the wrong time of year. Duncan, by hook or by crook, we've got to get him there and see if we can wheedle the truth out of him."

We hit upon a bait quite soon. Petemberson, we already knew, was a keen gardener. He had a little greenhouse and won prizes at local shows. Our bait was

63

a stack of flower-pots and seed-boxes still filling part of a stall, being too good to throw out. We got permission to offer them to Petemberson.

"Stack 'em in the drive and I'll take a look at 'em," he said, his casualness failing to hide an acquisitive gleam.

"Then we'd have to move them twice if you don't want them," said Duncan. "We really can't. We'll ask someone else."

That did it. After a bit of thought, he agreed to come.

As part of our plan we had put the ponies in the boxes to give atmosphere. In actual fact it went deeper: their presence might encourage Fermoy to come and play a leading part. In that we certainly succeeded!

The first thing Petemberson's eye fell on was the name plate which I had purposely propped up in a prominent place. All his muscles tightened.

"That was the plate that was pulled down," said Duncan. "We learnt the other day that because of an accident here Fermoy was shot."

"Wher'em the pots and boxes?"

"We would like to know what really happened," I carried on, standing in his way. "Can't you remember, Mr Petemberson?"

"I wasn't mor'n a nipper in those days. How should I know?"

". . . we really can't, we'll have to ask someone else . . ."

64

"But you said your uncle worked here," persisted Duncan in the face of the old man's mounting opposition.

"What if he . . ."

Petemberson broke off and went quite stiff as a loud whinny filled the building. Lyric gave a little whicker and stared eagerly into space. There was nothing to see, but plenty to feel, and it was all Fermoy. His presence filled the building.

Poor old Petemberson turned to do a bolt, but he seemed unable to take the steps that would carry him through the doorway.

"Did Fermoy kill your uncle?"

I hardly recognised Duncan's quivering voice.

"Nay, he killed nobot."

"Then why . . . ?"

The question went unfinished, for Petemberson's vocal chords seemed to take command of him.

"It was Tom Clark what died. The trap —there was one up there then"—and he nodded at the square hole into the loft, "it fell on him, knocking him off the steps so's he bashed his head on a corn bin what used to stand just there. Dead as a door nail, he lay. 'Twas Uncle Joseph put the blame on Fer— the hoss, for, see, he was larking in the loft and let the trap fall on Tom."

The atmosphere in the stable turned degrees colder and I shivered.

"So—so Fermoy was innocent?"

"Ay. He paid the penalty for Uncle."

"And your uncle told you afterwards?"

"Not him! He didn't know I seed it all. I'd no business on the place. I was on the scrounge for corn for me mum's hens. It weren't till later I heard about the hoss being shot. I was only a nipper when all's said an' done."

Petemberson gave a shake, as if freeing himself from the effects of a bad dream, and stumped out of the stable,

A grey horse stood in the yard.

minus the flower-pots. Duncan and I remained rooted.

"Poor, poor Fermoy!" I murmured.

Suddenly Conker, who had as usual stayed outside, uttered an appalled yell. A grey horse stood in the yard, head high and turned towards us, an animal of grace and breeding. As we looked, he just dissolved, but not before we had caught the glow in his full, dark eyes.

It was the first and last time we actually saw Fermoy, although I fancy Lyric from time to time communicated with him.

The next P.C. rally went off normally. Thanks to Fermoy having got us off to that good start, Lyric and I didn't feel at all screwed up and quite enjoyed ourselves. But, before that, the first thing we did was to put back Fermoy's name-plate over his box.

65

Pony Club Horse Trials Championships

The winning Fife team. Left to right: **Jane Hunter-Blair (17)**, **Jennifer Loin-Mitchell (15)**, **Diana Sprot (17)** *and* **Marjorie Watson (17)**.

Christine Burgess (18), *an individual competitor from the Carlow branch in Ireland, stood fifth in the Senior Individual Championship on Heathcliffe.*

Sally Cotton (17), *a member of the North Hereford branch, rode The Texan into second place in Section B of the Junior Individual Championship.*

Diana Sprot (17), who rode Pussy Galore for the winning Fife team.

Shirley King (17), an individual competitor from the Lamerton branch, riding Domingo.

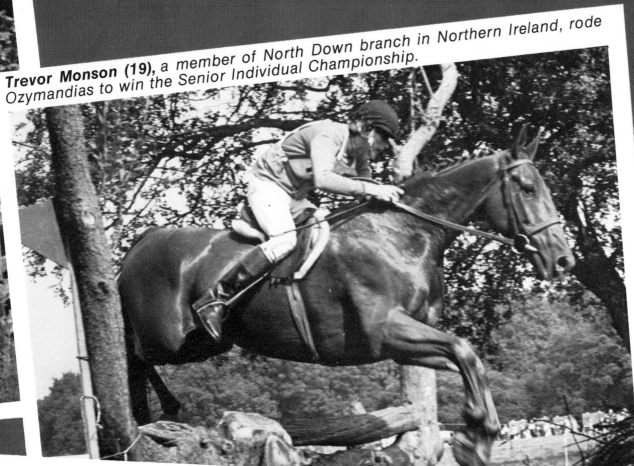

Trevor Monson (19), a member of North Down branch in Northern Ireland, rode Ozymandias to win the Senior Individual Championship.

Gail Scott (16) was runner-up in Section A of the Junior Individual Championship on Threepence; she was also a member of the Strathblane team which finished fifth.

Carolyn Blackwell (17), *the winner of Section A of the Junior Individual Championship, also rode Pepsi II for the Old Berkshire team which finished second.*

Carolyn Blackwell, born in 1956, made her first appearance at the final of the Pony Club Horse Trials Championships when she was seventeen. Riding Pepsi II, she won Section A of the Junior Individual Championship and also helped the Old Berkshire team into second place.

She had learnt to ride when she was ten, and was lucky enough to own her first pony at the age of twelve; two years later (in the autumn of 1970) Pepsi II was bought for her. The mare had some show-jumping experience with her former owner, Tina Brake, but it took time to bring her dressage up to standard. "We have always found this phase the most difficult," said Carolyn, "but after three years of hard work during the school holidays, things began to fall into place."

She is greatly indebted to the event rider Henrietta Knight. "We could never have managed without her. She has been tireless in her encouragement and advice since I was fourteen." It was Henrietta Knight who discovered Pepsi II in Somerset, and the mare has proved a wonderful find. In addition to the Pony Club success, she won a novice section of the adult two-day event at Windsor during 1973. She has also been successful in hunter trials, working-pony classes and show jumping.

According to her owner, Pepsi has "a mind of her own, but no vices. She loves competitions and hunting". Carolyn also loves these activities and, when she leaves school, she is hoping that she will be able to work with horses and continue to event. She derives great pleasure from bringing on young horses; she also enjoys sailing and skiing.

JAMES BUTCHARD

James Butchard, who was born in 1956, began riding at the age of four. He was a member of the Devon and Somerset branch of the Pony Club, but transferred to the Grafton in 1968 when his family moved to Hertfordshire. Some five years later he was chosen to compete in the Pony Club Horse Trials Championships for the first time and, riding The Virginian, he achieved the best overall score of the day to win Section B of the Junior Individual Championship.

The Virginian's owner, Philip Herbert, had outgrown the pony since riding him in the Championships the previous year; James Butchard was therefore invited to take his place. The new partnership was a tremendous success; from the five events in which they competed during the summer, they won no less than four first prizes.

Naturally, James is full of enthusiasm for The Virginian. "He has a lot of character but is very quiet in the stable. He is a super ride, very genuine and honest, great at dressage, bold across country and very clever at getting out of trouble when jumping. A fabulous pony!"

James is more experienced in dressage and cross-country riding than he is in show jumping; he therefore has to work particularly hard for the latter phase. During 1973 he had the help of the two Grafton instructresses, Mrs Cunningham and Mrs Watt; all his previous instruction also came through the Pony Club and he now holds his "B" Certificate.

Having taken his "O" levels, James left school last summer, with the idea of applying for a short service commission in the army. He also hopes for an opportunity to ride in races. His other interests include shooting, hunting and most forms of sport.

James Butchard (16), an individual competitor from the Grafton branch, rode The Virginian to win Section B of the Junior Individual Championship.

71

More

Moods

Limericks

As before, we are printing a small selection of the best limericks. There are many more which we liked, but it would be quite impossible to include them all. Consolation postal orders for 30p have been sent to the non-prizewinners in the 1974 competition whose limericks are published below.

There was an old pony in Ware,
The fillies all thought him a square,
  But when Donny starts singin',
  Old Pony gets swingin',
While flingin' his tail in the air.
          (by Fiona Sharp, 10)

There was an old pony in Ware,
Who gave children rides at a fair,
  For 2p a go,
  He'd go very slow,
But for 5p he'd run like a hare.
          (by Penny Whiting, 10)

There was an old pony in Ware,
Who grew such very long hair,
  That the family who bought him,
  Cried out, when they caught him,
"Tell us, are you stallion or mare?"
          (by Nichola Sincock, 13)

There was an old pony in Ware,
Who never took very much care,
  While jumping a fence,
  He got stuck in a trench,
And as far as I know he's still there!
          (by Kim Edwards, 13)

There was an old pony in Ware,
Who loved an eccentric bay mare,
  She sternly denied,
  That she'd run by his side,
And walked off with her nose in the air.
          (by Sarah Ashdown, 13)

There was an old pony in Ware,
Who closely resembled a bear,
  The reason was that,
  He grew very fat,
And also had very long hair.
          (by Catherine Gold, 13)

There was an old pony in Ware,
Whose back was like an armchair,
  His legs were all wonky,
  He brayed like a donkey,
And the times he stopped eating were rare.
          (by Heather Grossick, 11)

There was an old pony in Ware,
Once owned by a fat millionaire,
  It was with some misgiving,
  He gave up rich living,
And settled for plain, honest fare.
          (by Anne C. Wright, 14)

There was an old pony in Ware,
With an appetite exceedingly rare,
  First a bucket of rum,
  Then custard with plum,
To finish, a ripe juicy pear.
          (by Jenny Clay, 14)

There was an old pony in Ware,
Who decided to walk upon air,
  But his friends said "Get down!"
  And "You look a clown!"
So he promptly came down to La Terre.
          (by Joan Smith, 14)

There was an old pony in Ware,
Whose manners I just couldn't bear,
  He'd take a long drink,
  From the old kitchen sink,
Then dribble all over my hair.
          (by Sara Velate, 13)

There was an old pony in Ware,
Who stood on his head for a dare,
  It made him so dizzy,
  He got in a tizzy,
And leaped round the field like a hare.
          (by Philippa Michaelson, 14)

Clopper-clop, clopperty-clop, clop-clop. Big, bay, lumbering Shire-like Leo, with his shaggy mane, feathered legs and plates of feet, stepped unevenly but enthusiastically down the pot-holed tarmac drive to the farm. He was wondering, as he tugged at his bit, if there was going to be some polo after all, because this is where it all started for him the year before. So when he was untacked and turned into the paddock with the ponies who lived on the farm, he was all for enquiring about the polo; but of course they

A Polo Conversation

By Pauline Gerrard

Illustrated by Siân Williams

had to get their preliminary horsey introductions over first.

Wizard, the Welsh pony, was nearest to him. Leo trotted up to his old acquaintance who stood waiting with arched neck, the white blaze on his face a definite contrast to his brown body and legs. Wizard flashed a white-socked foreleg at the approaching Leo, who stopped dead once their noses were touching. "'Allo", "'alloo" they both squealed to each other, turned a complete circle in opposite directions, touched noses and squealed again.

Tall, rakish, all-thoroughbred Grouse cantered sedately up to them. He stood next to Wizard, their profiles merging; they were the same colour except that Grouse was devoid of any white. His "How-do-you-do" squeal sounded rather hollow, as if he had woken up with a sore throat that morning, but he had not, he always spoke like this nowadays since he had been hobdayed.

Winston, whose mother was a Welsh-cross arab and father was a thoroughbred, was rather more finely bred than either Leo or Wizard. He joined the others just as they began the next stage of the horsey introductions, a gallop to the end of the paddock. Wizard dropped his head and put in an almighty buck, Winston changed legs as he changed direction, Grouse did a perfect pirouette on his haunches and led the gallop to the other end of the paddock. Leo followed.

Eventually, they all stood quietly, head to tail, flicking the flies from each others faces. It was Wizard who started the conversation. "Why has that vicar brought you here again?" he wanted to know from Leo.

"It was real good fun," Leo chuckled.

"He's taken the family away for a few days, so your folk are looking after me," said Leo, adding hopefully, "I thought there might be some more polo."

Grouse neighed in that funny voice of his and said, rather snootily, "Why do you think there should be polo for you? You're not the right sort of pony at all, Leo; you should be pulling a cart or a plough."

"No one in the Pony Club seemed to

agree with your sort of thinking," said Leo, slightly aggrieved.

"Leo was really very good," Winston defended. "The man who took us in his lorry last year had a go on him, just sticking and balling, and said he was a real honest pony the way he put his heart into the game when he hadn't done it before and couldn't know anything about it."

"It was real good fun," Leo chuckled, "much better than the odd gymkhana."

"Why did they take you?" Grouse asked.

"Sarah took him instead of me," Wizard sulked. "She said I was getting hard to stop."

"And were you?" Grouse kept probing.

"Not for her."

"Maybe it was because of the way you behaved with that American the year before," Winston suggested.

"Why should that be? It's the way I behave with everyone else, and she knows it."

"What happened then?" Leo asked.

Winston could see that Wizard was not forthcoming, so he began the story himself. "That year there was a team of American students over here—I think they were from one of the best universities—and they played some of the teams in the senior tournament. Of course they hadn't any ponies, so on the first day they borrowed some of the ponies of the children who were playing in the junior tournament. One of our children lent Elf and she played very well for them. Now it was for obvious reasons that Sarah didn't lend Wizard."

Wizard turned his head away, trying to assume an air of boredom; he really didn't see why Winston should keep on so. Winston continued: "The next day the Americans played the Irish Guards on the best pitch. The Irish Guards could only lend the Americans six horses, so unless they could borrow two more they couldn't play the match straight off as there wouldn't be enough ponies to change for each chukka.

"They kept asking over the loud-speaker if anyone in the Pony Club would lend them two ponies for the match. Eventually Mrs Geer, who was in charge of us that year, went to the American manager and told him they could borrow Wizard and Darwin if they liked. I did hear her say, 'You won't thank me for it, but there are two ponies if you feel it necessary to have them.'

"Well," Winston took a breath, "the Americans did thank her for it in a very nice letter some days afterwards, but Darwin and Wizard only lasted one chukka. Both the players used spurs. If spurs are used on Darwin he just stands still and bucks, and anyone can guess what happens with Wizard. Mrs Geer did try to warn the Americans that Wizard was no problem to get going, but only a problem to stop. Only she said she didn't like to teach her grandmother how to suck eggs. Those students knew a great deal more about polo than she did."

"Yes," interrupted Grouse, "but they didn't know a lot more about Wizard."

"No," Winston continued, "because halfway through the first chukka the American got off Wizard and took his spurs off. He remounted and joined in the game. Darwin's rider kept his spurs on and, as the game galloped up the field, Darwin had all four feet firmly planted on the ground. Then the play turned the other way and the field started coming towards Darwin. Wizard suddenly noticed him a long way off, so he took hold of his bit and did one of his whizzy

Darwin just stands still and bucks.

acts straight across the pitch, overtaking the whole game and galloping straight past Darwin. In fact he almost disappeared, galloping flat out over a polo pitch and a half before the American could stop him. They decided to manage without the Pony Club ponies after that, even though it meant a gap between chukkas."

"Goes to show what I've been saying is right," grunted Grouse, "none of you chaps are really cut out for polo."

"Rubbish, man," Wizard insisted, "it was only because I saw my chance and took it. Sarah can manage me all right, and that other girl who played a chukka on me; I only got across half a polo pitch with her."

"Really," Winston insisted, "the standard of the Old Berks was improving that year. They were the only Pony Club team who were not attached to a polo club, and they were only bottom by two goals again. The trouble was all the other teams had improved too."

"It doesn't matter about being bottom," Leo insisted, "someone's got to be. The thing is to learn about the game, then, if any of them end up playing for the Irish Guards, they'll know something about it."

"Remember when we practised in Farmer Lane's field?" said Wizard. "His cattle had eaten the grass so bare that our children could twack the balls up quite a long way before they were stopped by a tussock of grass. The man who trained those Vale of Aylesbury teams that always won told our children the ball ran quite well enough, and that if they could play on that field with the ponies they had they could play anywhere."

"That's what the man from Kirtlington said about the gym horse they had to practise their sticking and balling on – if they could hit a ball on that they could hit it on anything."

"He was a good man. I remember when we were practising on the football pitch and Darwin was playing up, the cunning devil, so the man from Kirtlington got on him, determined to make him into a polo pony."

"That's exactly what he did do," interrupted Winston, "but, oh boy, Darwin did try and beat him. I've never seen him buck so much before or since, and we were all astonished at how that man managed to stay on."

"That was the first year we played," said Wizard. "The tournament was at Kirtlington Park, and the Polo Club allowed the Pony Club children to practise on Tuesday and Thursday afternoons in August."

"They practised at Kirtlington after that as well, when the tournament had moved to Windsor," Winston added.

"Didn't do them much good," grunted Grouse, "the Old Berks teams were always bottom."

"So what," said Leo. "They were good sporting children, and when they got those marvellous double orange rosettes with fourth prize written on them they were as pleased as could be."

"Sarah wanted to keep hers," said Leo, "but she felt she ought to give it to the Vicar. In the end, those kind people gave her a double white rosette with SPECIAL written on it; special for me, see?"

"Nonsense!" Grouse retorted. "Why wasn't there any polo in the Old Berks this year if everyone enjoyed it so much?"

"It's because most of the children who played before have sold their knock-about ponies and bought event horses, which they don't want to risk at polo. It's nothing to do with coming bottom. They found polo as much fun as anything else in the Pony Club. You don't always have to win just to enjoy something, Grouse."

"They weren't always bottom," Leo said. "At the end of that season the V.W.H. had a friendly tournament. There were six or seven teams, including two from the Old Berks, and our first team finished in second place."

"That's right," chipped in Wizard, "I was there as well." He and Winston and Leo all looked at each other, for they knew the real reason why the Old Berks first team had come second in that friendly tournament. At the end of the afternoon they had played the Old Berks second team, and managed to get three goals against them, thus pushing themselves into second place on the total goal scoring. But none of them intended to admit the whole truth. Grouse had been so snooty about the Old Berks polo, he could jolly well put the bare results into his disgruntled old pipe and smoke it!

My Horse

His eyes are kind and wide and bright,
His mane and tail are black as night.
Sleek and glossy that's his coat, his hoofs are also
    shiny,
He has a lovely sounding neigh, not a wheeze or
    whinny.
The rhythmic beat of his hoofs,
The steady, smooth way he moves.
The beauty of his grace and speed, as we fly over
    post and rail,
His arched neck, his rippling muscles, his flowing
    mane and tail.
As he watches the frolics of a hare,
His ears prick up, his nostrils flare.
Indignantly he snorts, and fretfully stamps his feet,
Pretending to be unobserved and almost obsolete.

By Jane Aspinal (Age 12)

CONTRIBUTIONS

The Editor will be pleased to consider any material (stories, poems, articles, puzzles, etc.) submitted for the next Pony Club Annual. Contributions, which must be the sender's own original work, should be sent to: The Editor, Pony Club Annual, Purnell Books, Berkshire House, Queen Street, Maidenhead, Berkshire SL6 1NF. Please state your full name, age and address when submitting material — ages refer to the time when contributions were written, not the date of publication. A fee will be paid for any contributions which are published in The Pony Club Annual. We regret that contributions cannot be acknowledged, but they will all be kept until January 11th, 1975, when the final selection will be made. Successful contributors will be notified as soon as possible after that date, and material which has not been selected will be returned to those who have enclosed a stamped, addressed envelope for that purpose.

CA—F

The Tetrathlon Championships is a relatively new Pony Club activity and one which has been warmly welcomed by all teenage boys and their parents, especially their fathers! Its object is "to encourage the all-round boy to further his interest in riding, and the horse generally by enabling him to combine his riding with other activities".

In the mounted games training the children have an introduction to team competition with a variety of actions centred round the pony—so it is a natural progression for the agile boy to enter the Tetrathlon field.

The Strathblane and District branch of the Pony Club are most fortunate to have several parents who are not only interested but also athletically inclined. Above all this we have Mrs Paula Gray, without whose perseverance and organising ability Strathblane would never have even started Tetrathlon training. In the spring of 1973 she wrote an article for our magazine explaining what the Tetrathlon is and what she had organised in the way of training. The enormous task of getting this new venture "off the ground", to a largely apathetic group of teenage boys, was left entirely to her. It is all very easy once a Pony Club has tasted success to "keep the ball rolling" so as to speak—it is quite another thing

to persuade sleepy fifteen- and sixteen-year-olds to get up out of bed to go swimming at eight in the morning, especially when cross-country running and shooting are their favourite sports and *not* swimming! In our case the early morning was the only time the Kirkintilloch baths manager could give us the use of his busy pool.

There are even more difficulties in Tetrathlon training than in other Pony Club activities. First of all there must be suitable grounds. We use Broadgate Farm, situated right in the centre of our district, where the shooting and training for cross-country running are combined, and where we have the use of a permanent cross-country riding course. June and John Dawson, who own Broadgate, are so generous and kind to every child, pony and parent that again we are uncommonly fortunate.

Secondly there is the equipment. You need a horse and all the tack, clothes and so on which are required for riding. You also need an expensive pistol and masses of ammunition; track suits and running shoes, plus the use of a swimming pool.

Thirdly there are the inroads on the children's time—trying to fit training in with normal school work and exams is

By Margaret L. Stuart

Tetrathlon

quite an art, although some children do swim, run and shoot at school.

Finally, finding the specialist trainers —more necessary now than ever before in this generation where "amateurs" rapidly become "professionals" to attain success. We in Scotland perhaps realise this more than our English friends who are used to fantastically high competitive standards.

Our trainers were deftly gathered together by Mrs Gray. Mr Sinclair, a champion pistol-shooting policeman, came to either Broadgate or Kirkintilloch, and had to start the boys from scratch, as none of them had even held an air pistol before. This was something that they could practise on their own, though great safety precautions had to be the rule. John Dawson, an excellent shot himself, kept a careful eye on the boys, not to mention the gun! The baths manager, Mr Orr, was most enthusiastic; he encouraged, advised and gave generously of his time all summer, so that we now have some very keen junior swimmers who previously could only ride.

Most of the boys had had some track training at school, so that this helped a little as far as the cross-country running was concerned. Again by good fortune one of our members' father, an ex-Rangers football player and school-master, is extremely interested in both orienteering and cross-country running. Bill Williamson liaised very closely with Mrs Gray and had panting parties of every age running around the farm fields in all weathers.

Broadgate Farm is hilly with lots of natural obstacles, which actually proved a disadvantage when we arrived at Stoneleigh, which has a flatter, more straightforward, open course.

With the close proximity of two riding clubs in the Strathblane District—the Allander and the Strathenderick—we have the advantage of not only Pony Club one-day events and hunter trials but also of joining in the adults' competitions when they include Pony Club classes.

There is always plenty of opportunity for the boys to ride over quite advanced cross-country courses. Fiona Rieve, our chief branch instructor, has been to Stoneleigh many times, both competing herself and as trainer of our inter-branch horse trials team.

The Area Inter-Branch Tetrathlon and Show-jumping were held over three consecutive days, which meant teams from a distance would only have to make one journey.

Owing to the novelty of Tetrathlon in Scotland there were only six teams competing and three of these were novice, as against nineteen teams in the Show-jumping Competition. This scene will surely change radically in the next few years, but Tetrathlon has to begin some-where.

Having qualified for Stoneleigh, we knew we should have to put in quite a bit more training so as to make the trip worth while. As with many of life's activities, just as we were enjoying our success at winning the area finals, we began to encounter some really bad luck! Our organiser had departed on a well-earned holiday when Peter Stirling, our strongest swimmer, and ex-mounted games stalwart, had his arm crushed in a nasty road accident. Then the horse of Stuart Walker, our cross-country riding "star", went lame. Some rather frenzied phoning took place and reserves were quickly put into the vacant places.

It might be pure coincidence, but look-ing down the boys' names who competed at Stoneleigh this year, Tetrathlon seems to be quite a family affair. There were two sets of brothers in the Strathblane camp, which was very useful for us since it cut down the transport costs.

The Tetrathlon Championships are run extremely efficiently and with the mini-mum of officialdom, which make the two days a delightful, informal experience.

For the spectator it is fascinating to see the competitors tackle such a variety of contrasting situations. Some of the boys were really "old men" of twenty, of course, which made the Strathblane team, averaging fifteen years, look like tod-dlers! Still, our Scottish appetites have been thoroughly whetted, and although our results at Stoneleigh were anything but brilliant, we shall be trying hard to return and do battle next year. Indeed we have some very keen and able eight-year-olds who have over a decade to follow in the present team's footsteps.

So often riding is looked on as a mainly feminine pursuit and to do the "manly" thing boys must play rugger and cricket, or take up mountaineering and skiing. This is especially the case in our area of Scotland where our Pony Club has no affiliated Hunt nor any tradition of point-to-point meetings which would otherwise cater for the keen, dare-devil, male teenager. Tetrathlon offers a worth-while challenge to these boys, a combina-tion of strength, technical skill, stamina and daring. Composite competitions will surely be the sports of the future. As indi-vidual performances become refined, room for improvement is rather limited; whereas in a combination of events there will be scope for bettering them for a long time to come.

My Mare

She canters on, among the trees,
Her head she shakes, her tail is twirled,
I watch her action, easy, smooth,
The finest mare in all the world.

Her colour's bay, her eyes are dark,
She stops to sniff the fallen leaves,
She starts, and pricks her well-shaped ears,
Imagines spooks among the trees.

She gallops on, a buck, a kick,
I love my mare more every day,
She lowers her head to eat the grass,
Perfect in every single way.

I walk across the fields of green,
My mare looks up, she loves me too.
I wish so much that she were real,
For I made her up, just for you.

By Deborah Smith (Age 15)

**Answers to
Reader's Crossword**
from page 37

Across
1. Dressage. 5. Aids. 7. Brand. 9. Tar. 10. Ergot. 13. Stable.
14. Hoof. 15. Drench. 17. Foal. 19. Lieu. 20. Yearling. 22. N.H.
23. Dog. 25. Lunge. 26. Fox. **Down** 1. Dartmoor. 2. Exercise.
3. Girth. 4. Badge. 6. Drag. 8. Bit. 11. Hay. 12. Gelding. 14.
Hunting. 16. Hounds. 17. Fly. 18. Tail. 21. Rein. 24. Off.

The winning Strathblane team. Left to right: **Irene Stephen (18)**, **Gail Scott (16)**, **Gary Brown (13)** and **Claire Lindsay (16)**.

Pony Club Show Jumping Championship

Joanne Vickery (17), a member of the New Forest team, riding Alah's Sash.

Sheila Martin (14), who rode Mowtown Spinner for the Four Burrow team.

Cairi and Grinn gaining third place in the 12.2 jumping at Hampton-in-Arden 1955.

From Warwick Fair

By Cynthia Muir

Cairi Muir first sat on a pony at the age of six weeks, so she can truly claim to have ridden all her life; her mount on this occasion was Jan, an eight hands Shetland pony which her mother had bought as a foal and owned for several years. Like all Shetlands Jan had tremendous character, and several of the habits of a dog, being quite accustomed to coming into the house and going upstairs, or lying down in front of the fire. Cairi and her younger sister, Corran, therefore literally grew up with a pony.

When she was fifteen months old Cairi made her debut in a show ring, riding Jan in a basket saddle, in a "most suitable pony" class. The pair did not win a prize, but they enjoyed this and sub-

sequent outings to shows to which Jan was conveyed, if the distance was too far for her short legs, in the family car, an ancient Austin 10. The front passenger seat was removed, mother, children, dog and picnic were all squeezed onto the back seat and Jan would then step in, to stand surveying the passing view calmly through the rear window, while Cairi's father acted as chauffeur. The family never paid a car parking fee; after all, if a vehicle carries a pony, it must surely be counted as a horsebox. . . .

As Cairi grew older, she rode Jan in a felt pad and became accustomed to helping with all the chores of feeding, saddling and tack cleaning. When she was three, her mother bought a black filly foal from the annual Warwick Pony Fair, for £7, feeling that this was the most economical method of having a pony when Cairi was of an age to ride more actively. The filly was probably straight off the Welsh hills and very wild, but Jan proved an excellent nanny and teacher; the new arrival was called "Grinn", which is Gaelic for "neat, pretty, shapely, beautiful", and she grew into a nice-looking pony. When the time came to break her in, at the age of three, she was so accustomed to being handled that she presented few problems and never showed the slightest fear of traffic.

Cairi was not one of those children who "get the bump" at a very tender age, but she achieved it at six years,

To Tidworth

riding a pony belonging to a friend who owned a riding school, and she developed quite a strong seat and was able, under supervision, to ride Grinn and to help with the pony's education. Grinn proved to be a real "bargain buy", and Cairi's first-ever rosette was won on her in an obstacle race at a little local gymkhana; soon after came a jumping prize. The rider was eight years old and the pony was five.

Luckily Cairi's home in Warwickshire was in a district where there has always been a great deal of equine activity, with shows ranging from the very small to County standard, and she was able to get a lot of experience in 12.2 jumping and at Pony Club rallies. Being small for her age, and having achieved some successes, she was asked to ride other people's ponies and did well with Ann Honigsbergen's 14.2 show pony, Only Me, when she was eleven. The next year she was asked to jump Jane, a 14.2 owned

by Jill Holmes, and had the pleasure of two firsts and a third in successive years at Hampton-in-Arden show.

Cairi was a keen member of the North Warwickshire Pony Club; she attended every rally to which she could possibly hack and went to camp as soon as she was old enough, a habit only broken in her late 'teens, when the demands of a job made this impossible. Another filly from Warwick Pony Fair had joined the family, meanwhile, a strawberry roan named Tiger Lily, and Cairi was largely responsible for her education. Tiger Lily was later sold and, with the money, a 14.2 named Rusty was bought, a chestnut who had had considerable experience in jumping. He was twelve years old and, when his owner was asked if she had hunted him, she replied with feeling: "Only once — he bucks!"

This was soon found to be an understatement and Cairi parted company

In 1957, Cairi and Rusty competed in a one-day event at the Windmill Hill Riding Academy.

several times with hounds, until she adopted the unorthodox method of getting off and running a little way with him, as soon as he started to play up. Surprisingly, this treatment worked and he became a really brilliant hunter who never turned his head at anything. He also had many successes at show jumping and dressage and took equally happily to Pony Club events. Twice he was chosen as a member of the N. Warwickshire team, but here luck ran out, for he was eliminated at a drop fence the first time, to Cairi's great distress, and, the next time, he went lame just before the day. Mr. John Tilke, of the Windmill Hill Riding Academy, near Stratford-on-Avon, gave invaluable help in training these teams.

Rusty was fortunate to be able to compete at all, for a day or two after he first arrived, a kick from another pony had cut a tendon and he was out of action for several months, a disappointment his young owner bore with great stoicism. She also rode for her Pony Club team on a friend's big, liver chestnut mare, Chocolate Time, which she show-jumped a little, and partnered a selection of

Cairi and Water Foam at the West Warwickshire Point-to-Point, 1959.

mounts in hunter trials and jumping; this variety of experience has been of great value to her and she added to it when she left school and worked for six months at a racing stable. She had a few rides point-to-pointing the next spring and loved the sport, but secretarial work in Birmingham did not allow her to continue with it.

Cairi married when she was twenty-two and by the time her sons, Dale and Michael, were born, she was living at Claverdon, near Warwick. Corran, also married, lived close by and together they ran a riding school, specializing in children, for a few years. Offered the choice of several young horses by a farmer friend, to school on, Cairi chose a very big, white-faced bay which she named "The Painter", and she hunted him and rode him in some horse trials. An extremely bold performer across country, he never really settled to dressage.

When he was sold Cairi was changing homes and was without a horse for a while. She is now living in Worcestershire and in 1970 her husband, John Dyson, a keen horseman, bought a four-year-old bay gelding by Troilus as a present for her. He was given the name "Truepenny" – "Ben" to his friends – and proved to be a quick-thinking ride, with obvious potential, having good action and a big jump. An unusual trait is his preference for a stable right away from other horses. Cairi hunted him a little and rode him for the first time in an event at Kilsby, in 1971, and at one other event that spring. In the autumn he competed at five horse trials, winning a seventh, two fifths and, at Holme Lacy, a first, before taking part in the Midland Bank Novice Championships at Wylye, an event for which only four five-year-olds had qualified. The cross-country day was wet, cold and windy, but he went extremely well, making nothing of the steep hills and impressive obstacles.

Ben was now an Intermediate horse and 1972 brought only minor placings in events; a fall on the flat at Tidworth, his first three-day trials, destroyed his chances, but he completed the event. Cairi rides him in some Foxhunter and Wing Newcomer classes, in which he has had successes, but show jumping is not his favourite activity.

In May 1973 he justified the faith which once caused Cairi to say: "There are lots of one-day eventers, but very few three-day horses, and I think Ben is one of them." After winning a two-day event at Wing he went to Tidworth where, in the Guineas section, he took the lead in

the dressage and increased it with a fast and accurate cross-country round. Despite penalties in the jumping phase, he had enough in hand to win comfortably.

Cairi trains Ben herself, at home, working him frequently on local hills, and she always attends Dick Stillwell's annual three-day course at Balsall Common. Only five feet tall, she has to carry so much lead in an event that, if she fails to swing the cloth up the first time, she has to get help to put it on when she saddles Ben. Dale and Michael care more for things mechanical than for ponies, but Cairi and John's three-year-old daughter, Claire, has her own Welsh pony and taught herself "the bump" when she was two. Perhaps one day she will follow in her mother's track.

Cairi and her Tidworth winner, Truepenny.

How to Draw Horses

By Christine Bousfield

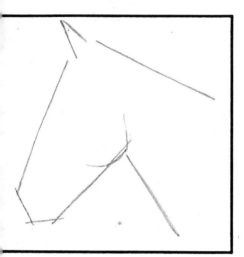

1

Drawing horses and ponies is something nearly all of us have attempted at one time or another; they make such interesting subjects, either as portraits or in motion.

The most important thing is to get the right proportions. One correct part drawn doesn't always fit with the other areas of the sketch. Let us take the head and try to show a simplified way of getting the correct size and proportions.

Start off with straight lines and circles. A profile is the easiest with which to start, other angles involve using perspective, areas farther away from you must be shown to recede to be correctly drawn. **(Fig. 1).**

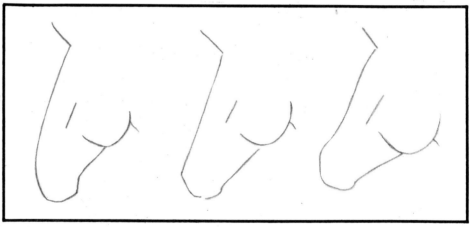

2

After this stage, note whether the subject has a Roman nose or a straight line from forehead to muzzle. Check to see if he has a small or large muzzle —in other words, where he differentiates from the so-called 'perfect horse' or pony. **(Fig. 2).**

3

Next, the sketch can be aided by a few more circles to show the right contours. The sketch shows a horse with a slight dip in his nose, usually where the nose band fits. Most horses have it. **(Fig. 3).** Ponies tend to have shorter heads, smaller muzzles and little ears, and seem wider across the cheekbone as a result.

92

4

5

6

The neck usually has a slight arch, unless the horse is in bad condition; ponies usually have shorter, thicker necks. **(Fig. 4)**. Draw in the final outline, showing main muscles and bony areas. These will be shown by shading. Certain features are always apparent as shown in the sketch **(Fig. 5)**. After that the main points of the particular animal can be drawn to give the actual character and personality. **(Fig. 6)**.

Most portraits are shown at rest, ears forward, or one flopped back, eyes open normally, or slightly closed for a sleepy look. A more alert pose is drawn if the horse notices something. The head and neck are held higher, ears well forward, the eyes wide open. If scared, the ears are back and the eyes can have a little white in the corner. Nostrils are flared, even to extreme, and the muscles stand out more, as do some veins. **(Fig. 7)**. The lips may be drawn back and the mouth opened.

7

8

When the pony turns his head towards you, the profile changes. One can see more of the other ear and eye and some of the nostril. The cheek area and lower lip and chin recede. Most of the front of the muzzle is shown. **(Fig. 8)**.

To understand the horse and pony, observe as many types as possible, and try to draw from life. Photos are useful to follow up sketches and see features in detail. Ponies may not stand still if they feel like eating or want to join the other ponies. Drawing them in their own box or stall with quick sketches, is the answer. Take a couple of sessions, the second allows you to spot mistakes done earlier. Finally, the pony's character is the most important point to capture, whether in a quick sketch or a detailed painting.

Test Your Knowledge

1. **When a horse is said to GO SHORT does he** (a) leave most of his food; (b) lack stamina; (c) move with shortened action or (d) fail to clear a water jump?

2. **Is a STRIPE** (a) a method of clipping; (b) a marking on the horse's nostrils; (c) a coloured browband or (d) a type of cross-country fence?

3. **Are CALKINS found** (a) on horseshoes; (b) in a pack of hounds; (c) on a sidesaddle or (d) in a horse's mouth?

4. **When a horse PECKS at a fence does he** (a) take off too late; (b) stumble on landing; (c) hit it with his hindlegs or (d) cat jump?

5. **Was the famous charger MARENGO ridden by** (a) The Duke of Wellington; (b) Alexander the Great; (c) Lord Kitchener or (d) Napoleon?

6. **Do LIPPIZZANER horses originate from** (a) France; (b) Poland; (c) Austria or (d) Russia?

7. **Do the initials B.H.S.I. indicate that a person is** (a) a qualified instructor; (b) a veterinary surgeon; (c) a hunter judge or (d) an official showjumping course builder?

8. **When a horse FINDS AN EXTRA LEG does he** (a) recover from lameness; (b) produce a sudden burst of speed; (c) perform a high school movement or (d) save itself after a bad jumping mistake?

9. **When a horse is FIRED is he** (a) put down; (b) eliminated from a competition; (c) treated for lameness or (d) failed in a veterinary examination?

10. **Was MISTER SOFTEE famous as** (a) a show jumper; (b) a three-day eventer; (c) a steeplechaser or (d) a show pony?

11. **If a horse were suffering from WARBLES would he** (a) make a noise when galloping; (b) have lumps on his back; (c) be unable to move in a straight line or (d) need to be warmed?

12. **Does a horse with BROKEN KNEES have** (a) a cracked bone; (b) faulty conformation; (c) scars as the result of an injury or (d) an open wound?

13. **When a horse is said to be BEHIND THE BIT does he** (a) wear a double bridle; (b) have a tendency to bolt; (c) refuse to be bridled or (d) evade any form of pressure on the bit?

14. **Does a horse with a GOOSE RUMP have** (a) a very long back; (b) a steeply sloping rump; (c) an inherent weakness in his back or (d) a large number of tiny spots?

15. **Does the term SPEEDY CUTTING refer to** (a) a leg injury caused by the horse's opposite foot; (b) low, straight action; (c) teeth which need rasping or (d) a method of clipping?

16. **Is the JOCKEY CLUB** (a) an association for all amateur riders; (b) one which protects the interests of professional jockeys; (c) the governing body for racing or (d) a type of whip? Answers on page 109

94

A Foal

A foal stands,
On spindly legs,
Beside a river.
His soft muzzle,
Testing the water,
Exploring.
The ripples nudged by his
Inquisitive nose
Scurry across the water
Like ripples in the sand.
He ventures,
The daring explorer,
Into the water and stands,
His little frame quivering
In excitement
And pride in his own bravery.
Then his head is thrown up,
His ears pricked and swivelling
Like radar,
To catch the whicker from
His mother,
Brought to him on the breeze.
He spurs his short,
Needle-fine legs,
To a graceful, flowing canter,
Interrupted with bucks and kicks
Of exuberance,
And meets the beautiful,
Brown, lithe mare.
The explorer home
From the danger
Of his own daring, adventurous
Spirit.

by Alison Saxby (Age 11)

Reader's Puzzle

by Karen Anne Lynn (aged 13)

Start at number one and work around the spiral, so that the beginning of each word is linked to the end of the one before. e.g.: ¹PELH²AM / B³LE/AD and so on.

P	A	L	O	M	I	N	O	R	W
d	d	L	e	a	T	H	E	r	e
a	H	b	r	e	d	a	d	S	G
S	G	o	L	G	a	l	m	T	I
O	U	V	S	P	O	l	i	O	A
O	O	O	G	T	T	O	r	N	N
L	r	i	O	L	O	P	a	E	G
a	o	r	O	N	i	B	L	W	L
P	H	T	t	e	k	r	a	m	O
P	A	a	r	r	a	b	a	r	A

CLUES

1. Golden horse
2. From Norway
3. Thoroughbred and Arab
4. Scottish island
5. A spotted horse
6. Riding seat
7. Attached to stirrups
8. Prince Philip Cup winners, 1964 and 1970
9. Flat-racing centre
10. Bred at 9
11. Once a famous horse of Alan Oliver's, also a butterfly
12. Pure white horse
13. A Russian trotting horse
14. A river in Russia
15. A fast pace
16. A game played on horseback
17. May often be jumped when hacking
18. What 5 is

Answers on page 109

Competition Results

The answers to the 1974 competition were as follows:

Olympic Riders and Horses
1. Ann Moore on Psalm
2. Harvey Smith on Summertime
3. Lorna Johnstone on El Farruco
4. Bridget Parker on Cornish Gold
5. David Broome on Manhattan
6. Mark Phillips on Great Ovation

Points for the Buyer
(Judged by Lt.-Col. W. S. P. Lithgow,
Executive Officer of the Pony Club)

1—D, 2—E, 3—A, 4—C, 5—F, 6—B

The results were as follows:
Seniors (aged 13 to 16): Winner: Jane Prior-Willeard (15), Oakwood Lodge, Ide Hill, Nr. Sevenoaks, Kent. **Runners-up:** Pegi Griffiths (13), Llymgwyn, Chwilog, Pwllheli, Caernarvonshire; Joan Smith (14), 187 Ovington Grove, Fenham, Newcastle upon Tyne, 5; Kate Gee (16), 'Heath Cottage', 95 Wimborne Road, Colehill, Wimborne, Dorset; Helen Emery (14), 14 Wardie Avenue, Edinburgh, 5; Pauline Saul (15), 30 Cambridge Street, Totterdown, Bristol BS3 4TG; Jenny Clay (14), Yew Tree Farm, Moulton Common, Near Spalding, Lincolnshire; Sarah Gellner (14), Old Litten Cottage, Froxfield, Petersfield, Hampshire; Linda Kite (13), 202 Andover Road, Newbury, Berkshire RG14 6NU; Nichola Sincock (13), Penpoll Farm, Porthkea, Truro, Cornwall; Kim Edwards (13), 26 Fort Road, Haslar, Gosport, Hants.

Juniors (aged 12 and under): **Winner:** Amanda Edwards (10), Wendover, Sharp's Lane, Horringer, Bury St. Edmunds, Suffolk. **Runners-up:** Kirsten Fleming (12), Cairbaan, Doune Road, Dunblane, Perthshire; Gwenda Wood (9), 6 Elm Garth, Roos, E. Yorks; Lesley Peek (10), 'West Grove', Langtongate, Duns, Berwickshire; Evelyn Claire Sanderson (12), Becketts Field, Bowden, St. Boswells, Roxburghshire; Joanna Percy (12), The Nook, Norwood End, Fyfield, Ongar, Essex; Alison Hale (12), Sunnylands, Berrow, Burnham-on-Sea, Somerset; Catherine Duell (12), Howden Hall, Durham Road, Stockton-on-Tees, Teesside; Carolyn Berkeley (12), 3 Meadow Court, Whiteparish, Salisbury, Wilts; Joanna Wilkins (11), Kymlea House, Gt. Staughton, Huntingdon; Belinda Norton (11), Higher Park Farm, Over Alderley, Macclesfield, Cheshire SK10 4SB.

"You look awful," said Melissa.

"I look terrifying," corrected Martin, reaching menacingly for his cardboard tomahawk. He and Patrick had painted red and white streaks across their faces, and wore pheasant-feather head-dresses.

Miss Jervens, the local Pony Club organizer, had drilled the five friends in their roles as "Indians" for the County Show, which included a "Western" Ride amongst its varied attractions—the main one was a demonstration of dressage by Monica Fuller, on the Three-Day Event champion, the ex-milk-cart skewbald, Muldoon.

To add "Indian atmosphere" they had painted white patches on the ponies, Patrick's black, Rebel, becoming a pie-bald, Rosemary's nervous chestnut mare, Tarantella, and Martin's bay, Traveller, skewbalds, and only Barbara's Fancy Fellow, born skewbald, and Melissa's Barbados, a glamorous palomino, had been spared. Traveller had managed to get his tail into a bucket of whitewash and had swished a startling pattern all over Martin's bare chest, adding to his alarming appearance.

"They'll think we are a circus when we ride to the show," said Rosemary, a trim Indian maiden in her mother's suede waistcoat, her long, black (wool) plaits braided with coloured ribbons.

"Proper Indian maidens walked," said Patrick loftily. "Only braves had ponies; it's all women's lib, letting you ride at all. You ought to plod along behind your brave's pony!"

"I would have tickled mustang with pointed stick and watched Indian brave biting dust," said Barbara flatly.

"We are all much too early," said Rosemary. "I knew we would be. What are we going to do? Hang about here for an hour, or go to the show and frighten the spectators—but that would spoil the surprise."

"Do you think Monica Fuller will be giving Muldoon a work-out this morning?" asked Melissa. "They are staying with Mrs ffrench-floss, aren't they? Perhaps we could go and watch. Felicia was carrying on about it last time I saw her. You'd think *she* was the Three-Day Event champion, to hear her."

Hearing hooves, Martin peered over the hedge and groaned. "You can ask her. Here she comes."

Felicia ffrench-floss, whose opinion of her riding ability was shared by no one except her mother—who spared no expense to mount her daughter on the best horses money could buy—was the most unpopular member of the local Pony Club branch.

Trouble

By Carol Vaughan

Illustrated by Sally Webb

"A painted face and feathered headband."

"I say," said Felicia, reining in her elegant grey mare, Lady Luck. "It's jolly lucky I caught you. Something awful's happened!"

"It's all been cancelled," said Patrick in sepulchral tones. "I saw it in the tea-leaves this morning—disaster, disaster, disaster!"

"You all drink coffee in your family," said Rosemary prosaically.

"Stop being so silly," said Felicia impatiently. "It's important. Muldoon has disappeared. The stable door was wide open this morning. The groom and I have searched all the home paddocks, but he's not there. Monica Fuller's frantic. Miss Jervens came to see her. She told me to try to catch you, to tell you to go to the show by different routes, covering as much ground as possible, in case he has just strayed."

"I've only seen him in photographs,"

said Melissa.

"It shouldn't be difficult," said Rosemary. "He's a skewbald, close to 16 h.h.—there can't be that many around."

"Let's split into teams of two," said Patrick. "We can cover more ground that way. Felicia, you had better come with me," he added, resignedly. He knew, from experience, that she did not get on with any of the girls and Martin always teased her until she lost her temper. "I suggest that Martin and Barbara team up, and Melissa and Rosemary. That gives us three directions to cover."

The next few minutes were a heated

geographical discussion on routes and likely places.

"We had better start," said Rosemary. "There isn't that much time. Good luck!"

Felicia rode off beside Patrick, smirking at the other girls, triumphant that Patrick had chosen *her* as his partner, much too conceited ever to guess the real reason. They had a short canter along a lane and came out on the Blasted Oak Heath — named after a lightning-struck tree.

"We had better separate and search each side of it," said Patrick, glad to have a respite from Felicia's tiresome chatter — always about herself. "We'll meet at the ford."

"All right," said Felicia importantly. "I bet I find him."

Patrick kept Rebel to a hand canter, keeping a sharp watch for any movement — a brown and white horse under the trees lining the common would be camouflaged by leaf shadow — watching, too, Rebel's ears, a sure sign if the pony spotted something unusual. His feathered head-band slipped and he pushed it up impatiently; he grinned, wondering what he looked like, with painted face, feathered-head and a moth-eaten moleskin waistcoat flapping over his bare chest.

There was a noise in the trees to his left and Rebel threw up his head, snorting. Patrick reined in. He thought he saw something move. Was that a cry, a distant cracking of branches? Turning, he rode towards the trees, Rebel advancing with the cautious gait of a horse ready to swing round and bolt if it sees danger.

"Muldoon!" exclaimed Patrick, in surprise. "That must have been the thief, running for it, that I heard."

The large skewbald horse was standing under a tree, a halter rope swinging free under its chin; there was no sign of the person who had cried out. Riding forward, talking reassuringly, Patrick grabbed at the halter rope; the horse looked at him curiously.

"Come on, Muldoon," said Patrick, turning and riding back to the heath. "That was easy enough. You'll be at the show in plenty of time."

Cantering down the slope to the ford, Patrick heard a loud whinny, and laughed. So Felicia was already at the rendezvous, after her fruitless search. What a surprise for her!

Reaching the clearing, Patrick reined in with a jerk. Felicia was waiting — holding an identical skewbald.

"I've found . . ." began Felicia importantly, but then, squinting against the sunlight through the leaves, she saw Patrick's skewbald. "Where did you get that one?" she asked. "*I* found Muldoon by the river. I don't understand . . ."

Patrick began to laugh. "But which *is* Muldoon? One of us has pinched someone else's horse."

"Mine's Muldoon," said Felicia crossly; she had been picturing herself as the heroine of the hour.

"I'll toss you for it," said Patrick. "Short of holding an impromptu Three-Day Event, I don't see how we can decide. Come on, to the Police Tent at the County Show. Let's hope they'll have a horsey Sherlock Holmes to sort it out."

Martin and Barbara rode for so long without seeing a single horse that Barbara finally said she thought there had been a clean sweep by the horse-thieves; it wasn't only Muldoon they had taken!

"Don't be an ass, they are all at the show," said Martin.

"Oh, I hadn't thought of that," said Barbara, feeling foolish. "I wonder if the

"Mine's Muldoon."

others have had any luck?"

"We shan't know that until we reach the show—unless we find Muldoon," said Martin. "I wonder if there's a reward . . ."

"Look!" said Barbara.

A gypsy encampment on the scrap of wasteland was surrounded by grazing horses and ponies, some tied up, some hobbled. The big skewbald was standing by the hedge, leaning over the ditch to nibble at the leaves, his halter rope swinging from a broken branch.

"I say," breathed Martin. "Nobbled by the gypsies! What a scoop for us! How are we going to rescue him?"

"We should fetch the police," said Barbara nervously.

"What, and have them spirit away the horse before we get back?" asked Martin impatiently. "You know how clever gypsies are with horses; he'd be dyed brown and in the next county before the local policeman had finished filling in a

. . . hitting Muldoon on the rump . . .

report. We have to take him now—he's already broken loose, so he's technically a stray—Monica Fuller needs him this afternoon, not next week."

"But that's stealing," squeaked Barbara.

"Nonsense," said Martin. "It's reclaiming lost property. Quite different."

"But we can't just walk up and take him. Someone in those caravans would be sure to notice," objected Barbara.

"I have a plan," said Martin. "Remember, we're Indians. I'm going to crawl up that ditch, grab the halter rope and crawl back, very slowly, towing the horse behind me, keeping his head down, as if he's grazing. You hold the ponies in that lane, ready for the getaway. At the end of the lane there is a little copse, off to the left, leading up to the Market Hill road, the quickest way to the show-ground."

Barbara shuddered with horror, her mouth dry, but she was not going to let Martin say that girls were useless in emergencies. Starting at every sound, the distant rattle of a saucepan in a caravan, the irritable bark of a dog, the snort of a horse, she waited while Martin slithered off down the lane, feathers rippling down his back. Some ten minutes later Martin suddenly appeared, running, dragging a reluctantly trotting Muldoon behind him.

"Quick," he said. "One of the men has just come out of the caravan. I think he saw . . ." Thrusting the halter rope into her hand, he grabbed Traveller's reins and vaulted into the saddle with a lithe grace any Red Indian might have envied, war-whooping and hitting Muldoon on the rump with the flat of his hand, as there was an angry shout at the end of the lane.

"He's seen us!" choked Barbara, clinging on for dear life as Fancy Fellow shot off down the lane, his ears back, snapping at the galloping skewbald

102

beside him, all three of them all-but bolting.

"He's after us; he's got one of the other horses," shouted Martin. "Quick, turn for the copse; we'll jump the stile and hope he doesn't see where we turned off."

Barbara gulped, wishing herself anywhere else, pulling Fancy Fellow's head round to the sharp turn, dragging Muldoon behind her. The stile loomed ahead. Fancy Fellow's ears pricked; he gathered himself to jump. Muldoon balked and the halter rope slid painfully through her fingers, almost pulling her out of the saddle, so that she jumped with an exaggerated backward seat, like an old-fashioned sporting print, but Fancy

Fellow, a solid pony, cleared the obstacle in spite of her and they were flying through the copse. Behind her there was a loud shout and a crash and then Muldoon was racing up beside her. Reaching out, she caught the halter rope. Risking a glance behind her, she could see no sign of Martin—but perhaps he had taken the other path through the copse, to mislead the pursuit.

Reaching the heavy gate onto the road, Barbara dismounted and led Fancy Fel-

"Where did you get that one?"

103

low and Muldoon through, holding it open for Martin, in case the gypsy was still in close pursuit.

Martin appeared quite suddenly through the trees, holding Traveller to a collected trot, a large skewbald horse trotting at his side.

Barbara's eyes widened. "Where did you get that one?" she gasped. "Martin! You can't steal *all* the skewbald horses in the county. You'll be in prison for years. They can't *both* be Muldoon!"

Martin gaped in amazement. "I thought it was the same one," he said. "I thought it had got away from you. When it didn't jump with you, I shouted and it took off from a standing start and went over, but that put off Traveller. I had to put him at it again, and I took the other path, just in case you had missed Muldoon. And I found him. At least, I thought I had."

"Let's go quickly to the police station,"

said Barbara weakly. "This sort of thing makes me nervous. I don't like being on the wrong side of the law!"

"We are not on the wrong side," said Martin defensively. "We are rescuing Muldoon."

"How many Muldoons are there?" asked Barbara.

"If we find him it'll be a triumph for the superiority of the female brain," said Rosemary.

"I don't feel very superior," said Melissa. "I was always hopeless at all those guessing games we had to do when we went to children's parties; you always won everything."

"Reason it out," said Rosemary, ignoring this. "Two things could have happened. He has strayed or he has been stolen. Which is the most likely?"

"You tell me," said Melissa resignedly. It was never any good interrupting Rosemary's thought processes.

"You young varmints."

"If he has been stolen by professionals, he is miles away in a horse-box," said Rosemary. "And we shall never find him, but if he has only strayed, he might have been shut in a field by a helpful passer-by, or 'rescued' by a kind old lady, or stolen by a local thief . . ."

This list of solutions seemed endless, but when they reached the main Market Hill road, after an exhaustive search all along their route, they had seen no skewbald horse. . . .

A police car swept past them and stopped on screeching tyres. Tarantella danced backwards, snorting nervously; Rosemary leant forward to pat her neck, bringing up a cloud of dried whitewash.

"There they are! Indians! What did I tell you? Officer, arrest them at once!" cried a large lady in magenta slacks and a yellow shirt, bursting out of the police car. "Frightening my poor little Amanda, attacking her, stealing our horse . . ."

"Now then," said Sergeant Jenkins, of the Market Hill police. "What's all this? This lady, Mrs Farringdon-Smith, says her horse was stolen by Indians from a copse off Blasted Oak Heath. I had some difficulty in believing her, but now . . ." He paused, taking in their "fancy dress" with a twinkle in his eye. "It's Melissa Green and . . . Rosemary Straker, isn't it? I know the ponies. Now, what's been going on?"

Rosemary and Melissa exchanged glances and began to giggle. That seemed to enrage Mrs Farringdon-Smith even more; she gobbled at them like a turkey.

"We . . . we haven't been near the Heath," said Rosemary truthfully. "Er . . . what colour was the horse?"

"It was a brown and white horse, like something out of a circus," cried Mrs Farringdon-Smith. "I hired it with a gypsy caravan for a week to take the kiddies for a holiday and Amanda begged to be allowed to lead it to the river for a drink. And what happens? She is attacked by a horrible Red Indian and comes screaming back to the caravan to fetch her brother, Adrian. But when he goes to look, the horse has gone. And the Indian."

Sergeant Jenkins sighed. "First two circus horses are reported missing, after the road accident to the horse-box—one had to be destroyed, broke a leg, poor brute, and then Mrs ffrench-floss reports a champion riding horse strayed or stolen from her stables, and now this. What a day!"

"I am afraid that there has been a slight mistake," said Rosemary. "We were out looking for the champion riding horse, with friends of ours, but I can't understand why . . . why Amanda didn't *say* that it was her horse."

"Well, as to that, she didn't actually *see* the Indian take the horse," said Mrs Farringdon-Smith huffily. "Naturally she was so frightened that she ran away when she saw the Indian."

"So the 'Indian' just found an abandoned horse," said Sergeant Jenkins, his brow clearing.

"But that doesn't change anything," cried Mrs Farringdon-Smith. "I want my horse back. Officer, aren't you going to arrest these . . . savages. They are in the same gang."

"Don't see how I could load the ponies into the police car, madam," said Sergeant Jenkins, winking at the children.

"You'll find him at the show," said Melissa helpfully. "We are all meeting at the Police Tent."

Sergeant Jenkins roared with laughter. "Doesn't sound much like a gang to me," he said. "We'll be off."

"But none of them is Muldoon."

"How could Patrick and Felicia have made such a mistake?" said Melissa.

"If you are looking for a skewbald horse—and you find one, loose—I don't suppose you stop to ask questions," said Rosemary reasonably. "Especially when there is no one to ask!"

"Come on," said Melissa. "There's still hope for us—Muldoon is still missing, if they have found a double . . ."

"A ringer," said Rosemary.

"Don't be so technical," said Melissa. "A double is good enough for me—double trouble!"

Long black plaits swaying behind her, Rosemary led the way along the grass verge of the road to Market Hill, in the wake of the police car, still keeping her eyes open for stray skewbalds.

As they passed a gate a wild cry startled the ponies; Tarantella's plunge nearly unseated Rosemary. A fierce-faced, dark-eyed man, with a mop of untidy black hair, astride a raw-boned chestnut horse, was glaring at them across the gate.

"You young varmints!" he yelled. "Indians! Horsethieves! I'll . . ." But he was speaking to thin air. The two ponies were streaking down the road, needing no urging from their horrified riders. A loud, bellowing roar followed them; Melissa risked a look over her shoulder and gasped.

"Golly, he's coming through the hedge! Quick, Rosemary. He's dangerous! Whatever has happened now?"

"I don't know, and I'm not stopping to

ask," said Rosemary tersely, all her attention on trying to keep the nervy chestnut mare from bolting. "If we cut across the green at Shepherd's Corner we can jump into the showground over that hedge and hide in the Police Tent. He won't dare to follow us there."

"I'm not so sure," said Melissa, shivering in spite of the blazing sun. "I think he's lost a skewbald horse, too!"

The Police Tent at the County Show had been intended as a public service, help for lost children and a headquarters for the Police Car Driving Demonstration—not a cross between a Red Indian pow-wow and a circus.

Four large skewbalds stood in front of the tent, towering over the three "pinto" ponies, though only Fancy Fellow still looked "real", the others having faded to roan splodges, and Lady Luck, still immaculately grey.

Mrs Farringdon-Smith was sitting on a stool fanning herself with a programme and staring, cross-eyed, at the four horses. Monica Fuller was holding her sides and rocking with laughter, as the last two "Indians" arrived, and joined the line-up of exotic-coloured horses.

"But none of them is Muldoon," she said. "Not one of them. I can't imagine . . . I didn't know there were that many skewbalds in fifty miles!"

"And I don't know which is mine," wailed Mrs Farringdon-Smith. "I didn't know I should have photographed him, or taken his hoofprints. I should have stuck to motor caravans; at least they have numbers at both ends."

Half the horse-show spectators had abandoned the thrilling tension of a Hack Class to come and watch the Wild West Circus outside the "sheriff's" tent, giving applause and misguided advice, until they were scattered by the arrival of an avenging figure on a bony chestnut, tearing across the grass, elbows and knees flapping, hair flying in the wind.

"I want my horse," he cried.

"It—it was all an awful m-mistake," stammered Martin, stepping forward bravely. "I'm frightfully sorry, sir, but . . ."

"My horses! My beauties! My lost ones!" cried a voice, as a man wearing a midnight-blue jacket with CIRCUS embroidered on it, in gold, came rushing through the crowd. "But who are these? Where do they come from? A perfect match! Can one be for sale, to replace my tragically dead Pluto?"

"For sale?" echoed the gypsy, stepping forward, a gleam in his eye, pushing Martin out of the way. "If you're looking for a top-class horse, mister . . . You don't often see a horse like mine," he added, inaccurately.

A stir was caused by a new arrival, which drew a cheer and a round of applause from the spectators.

Across the field, at full gallop, came a gypsy caravan, swaying and lurching, driven by a boy of fifteen, feet braced on the footboard, trying to hold the racing skewbald horse.

"Adrian!" shrieked Mrs Farringdon-Smith shrilly.

"Mum! I've found him," cried the boy, coming to a dramatic halt as the skewbald saw the crowd in front of him at the last moment.

He flung up his head and sat down on his hocks, snapping at a shaft and nearly overturning the caravan.

"Muldoon!" cried Monica Fuller. "It's Muldoon!"

Thirsty Weather

Answers to Puzzles

Test your Knowledge
from page 94

1. (c) move with a shortened action
2. (b) a marking on the horse's nostrils
3. (a) on horseshoes
4. (b) stumble on landing
5. (d) Napoleon
6. (c) Austria
7. (a) a qualified instructor
8. (d) save itself after a bad jumping mistake
9. (c) treated for lameness
10. (a) a show jumper
11. (b) have lumps on his back
12. (c) scars as the result of an injury
13. (d) evade any form of pressure on the bit
14. (b) a steeply sloping rump
15. (a) a leg injury caused by the horse's opposite foot
16. (c) the governing body for racing

Reader's Puzzle
from page 96

1. Palomino
2. Norwegian
3. Anglo-Arab
4. Barra
5. Appaloosa
6. Saddle
7. Leathers
8. Atherstone
9. Newmarket
10. Thoroughbred
11. Red Admiral
12. Albino
13. Orlov
14. Volga
15. Gallop
16. Polo
17. Logs
18. Spotted

COUPON
PONY CLUB ANNUAL
COMPETITION
1975